A LANCASHIRE BORDER WALK

Silver Link Publishing Ltd
The Coach House, Garstang Road, St Michael's on Wyre, Lancashire PR3 0TG

Cover Photograph: From Downham Village looking towards Pendle in Summer 1988.
Norman Duerden

CONTENTS

This book is dedicated to the memory of

JAMES HILTON

the talented Leigh author of 'Lost Horizon,' 'Goodbye Mr Chips,' and 'Random Harvest,' and a favourite uncle of mine.

Copyright Howard D. May/ Silver Link Publishing Ltd, 1988.

First published in the United Kingdom, June 1988.

Imagesetting by Ps & Qs, Liverpool. Printed in the United Kingdom by The Amadeus Press, Huddersfield, Yorkshire.

May, Howard
   Lancashire border walk : walking the old Lancashire county border.
   1. Lancashire - Visitors' guides
   I. Title
   914.27'604858

ISBN 0-947971-20-3

ACKNOWLEDGEMENTS

I would like to express my sincere gratitude to the Tourist Information Centres at Barley, Clitheroe, Hebden Bridge, Nelson, Rochdale, Rossendale and Saddleworth, whose assistance in compiling the list of overnight accommodation was invaluable. I am also indebted to County Planning Officer, David Tattersall BA MCD FRTPT, at Lancashire County Council Offices, Preston, for the mountain of helpful literature he kindly forwarded at my request.

Special thanks are also due to the farmers and landowners on whose land I inadvertently trespassed during the course of locating lost and forgotten footpaths, all of whom met the offence with understanding and in certain instances went to extreme lengths to point this wayfarer in the right direction.

To the numerous individuals en route along the old Lancashire county boundary who kindly provided refreshments, improved my route and befriended this occasionally unkempt stranger and backpacker, I will be forever grateful. Their sense of humour, amicable banter, and profound interest in my journey made the walk that much more enjoyable.

Friends also played their part, offering encouragement and advice in their own particular special interests. In this respect I convey my thanks to Pauline Mellor and Charlie Owen; thanks also go to my friends and next door neighbours, James and Miriam Platt, for keeping a watchful eye on my home during periods of long absence.

A very special word of thanks is due to William D. Amos, former editor of *Lancashire Life*, magazine, for without his patience and perseverence in editing my inexperienced scripts of yesteryear, I would quite probably have consigned my typewriter to the dustbin!

Finally, I would like to thank Silver Link Publishing Ltd. for the professional way in which they have conducted their part of the production. I now regard them as friends, rather than simply my publishers.

Howard May,
Leigh, Lancashire, 1988.

Author's Note

A good map is an essential requirement for the Lancashire border walker, and to make the best of the route, I would advise use of the Ordnance Survey *Landranger* 1:50,000 series. You will need sheet numbers: 89, 90, 96, 97, 98, 102, 109 and 110.

FOREWORD
by
MIKE HARDING

LANCASHIRE as a county has been much written about, mainly in historical or geographical terms however, and it is rare that you find a book describing a trip like this. Howard May's book is a guide for walkers, describing a trip along the old county boundary, but it is also informative and entertaining. It is a book that has fascinated me, not just because of the author's obvious love of landscape, but also because of the interesting details he has managed to unearth about every nook and cranny along the way.

Over the years I have walked in a few of the places mentioned in these pages and reading it now has made me want to go back there and look at it all again in the light of the stories and detail that abound in *A Lancashire Border Walk.*

Former President: Ramblers Association.

INTRODUCTION

IT must be all of ten years ago that I first realised the potential of the old Lancashire county boundary as a new long-distance footpath, although it was only in 1986/87 that I finally put procrastination behind me and tackled the venture. I had often glanced at the 1:50,000 Ordnance Survey maps of the old boundary, and how public rights of way connected one with the other from Mossley, near Manchester, to the Duddon Estuary in Furness, a distance approaching 270 miles.

Lancashire's old county boundary does, of course, begin where the River Mersey meets the Irish Sea, following the course of the Manchester Ship Canal and the River Mersey to

Above: The Lancashire landscape as seen from the Low Road below Longridge Fell, revealing the Hodder Valley, looking towards Waddington. In the distance is Bradford Fell.

Stockport, Cheshire, where it deflects via the River Tame through Dukinfield, to seek the uplands above Mossley. A major obstacle prevents this stretch of boundary from being completed, in that the Manchester Ship Canal Company owns most of the land through which the route runs, making it private property. However, this section of the old boundary is also heavily industrialised and therefore of rather less appeal to those in search of the beauties of

Right: A peaceful image of a Lancashire village. This picture shows Waddington Brook trickling through the hamlet which takes its name.

rural Lancashire. In consequence, our route begins at Mossley, and passes through the bleak, gritstone high country of the southern Pennines via Standedge and Blackstone Edge before crossing Summit Pass and the Cliviger Gorge to Boulsworth Hill. We then move through the Forest of Trawden, Wycollar and Laneshaw Bridge. Now the old boundary makes an acute turn to the west, pushing through Pendle witch country to pick up the Rivers Ribble, Hodder and Dunsop for a journey across the peaks of Bowland Forest. Come the northerly termination of Bowland, Lancashire 'sticks out its tongue' to join the old country boundaries of

Westmorland and Yorkshire at the 2,250 feet summit of Great Coum, in the Yorkshire Dales National Park, from where it descends on the splendid limestone lowlands of Kirkby Lonsdale, Hutton Roof and Silverdale. The old boundary now fords the Kent Estuary to kiss the easterly shoreline of the beautiful Cartmel Peninsular, where it heads north into the Lake District National Park, crossing Lake Windermere at High Cunsey to pursue the lake's western shoreline, to Ambleside. Finally, the old boundary flows with the Rivers Brathay and Duddon, via the remote and forbidding Wrynose Pass, and encircles Furness, whence it leaves *terra-firma* in the Duddon Estuary, close to Foxfield. How could such a magnificent walk fail to satisfy the seeker of wild solitude, sustain the adventurous soul or lift a city-weary heart?!

During the walk we will cross 26 rivers, pass through 71 villages, tread the soil of 3 National Parks, observe around 110 species of birds and enjoy a pint or two of ale in several of the many country inns *en route*. We will also become acquainted with the characters and country ways that have for generations shaped Lancashire's magnificent border country, and discover that inexplicable happenings in the supernatural world and age-old superstitions are still a part of everyday life in the bleak uplands, where the late 20th century has exerted little influence on the country folk.

From the ghostly cavalier that reputedly haunts a Pennine inn, to a moorland farmers wife receiving a visit from the Grim Reaper, and from hound trailing and char fishing to grouse shooting and shrimp fishing, all the old mysteries and traditional ways of life are still very much in evidence, for those who wish to seek them out.

It would, of course, be foolish of me to suggest that nothing had changed along this route in recent times. Tourism is 'booming' throughout the length of the old Lancashire county boundary we shall explore. Far from being a blight, as perhaps some folk would have you believe, tourism both provides much-needed employment to residents of remote districts, and also helps to conserve the countryside

Above: Waddington is one of my favourite Lancashire villages, which is why I have featured photographs of it with this introduction. This is Saint Helen's Well, in the village churchyard, from which local people communally drew their water each day, before the arrival of piped water.

7

and its ancient traditions. What would happen, for example, to rush-bearing festivals, game fairs and agricultural shows if the financial backing of tourism wasn't there to lend its support? On a less positive note however, tourism has had (for me, at least) a drastic effect on many of our traditional country inns, particularly those of the Lake District National Park, where many are no more than licenced restaurants. In many cases,these old inns are now devoid of local residents, who along with their darts, dominoes, skittles and all, have seemingly been pushed aside in a mad scramble to earn the coin of the realm.

The changing face of agriculture and its over-dependence on chemical fertilisers nowadays has also had a detrimental effect on the countryside, the most adversely affected areas being valley pastures, where silage production demands that so much nitrogen be used on the land that little else (other than grass) can sustain an existence. The price of mutton does indeed extend way beyond the rim of the purse. On the whole however, the countryside of Lancashire's old border country is in healthy condition, and the landscape is improving all the time, for in recent times conservationists are heeded more than in the past, when they were often regarded as prophets of doom.

I hope this book also illustrates a more compassionate side to human nature than that reported by the daily press; to show that many human-beings are helpful and honest to the core. 'Backpacking' in unfamiliar surroundings occasionally calls for assistance and co-operation from total strangers to solve one problem or another, be it directional information or permission to camp for the night on private property. In today's crime-ridden society, strangers can be greeted with a great deal of apprehension, particularly in small, remote communities, who obviously feel more vulnerable than most. The answer lies in explaining what you are doing, and why, to those from whom you require assistance. More than once my maps were spread out on a bar-room floor, my route being scrutinised and amended by local 'tipplers' eager to see that I pursued the most interesting paths from their village. People love to be involved, just as much as they hate being left 'in the dark.'

And finally, to the purpose of the book. My sincere wish is that *A Lancashire Border Walk* first and foremost portrays a picture of the Lancashire county border countryside, its people and their way of life, as observed in the late 1980s. In consequence, the book is intended for those who would rather see and experience Lancashire's old border country, rather than simply pass through at break-neck speed – although this does not prevent the seasoned athlete (or walker with fire at his heels!) from attempting the route! If I have achieved this, then I have succeeded; if not, then I must try again.

So, walk with me through the following pages, illustrated with my own photographs, to discover a Lancashire border country filled with fascination, where we will pursue routes first initiated by our prehistoric ancestors, tread the pavement laid down by the packhorse drover, and saunter through a time-forgotten landscape that both would still recognise.....

Howard May,
Leigh, Lancashire, 1988.

Chapter 1:
WALKING THE EDGES

OUR walk along Lancashire's old county boundary begins at Mossley railway station, a small station set hard by an uplift of moor and, like its neighbouring station at Greenfield, much prone to the ravages of winter blizzards. To locate the old county boundary from the station's exit, turn right (or south) along the hamlet's main street and then first left around the dog's leg bend, continuing down the gradient to the stream and another sharp bend. From here, it is a simple 'follow-your-nose route', although if in doubt, ask for the whereabouts of popular Micklehurst Cricket Club. Incidentally, ignore the Micklehurst indicated on the Ordnance Survey map, which is in the wrong direction for our purposes!

Once out of the dip of the stream and around the bend, our route towards the eastern hills comprises uphill walking of the leg-aching variety, and so it remains until we reach the 1,700 feet summits of Hoarstone Edge and Wilderness. By the way, it never fails to astound me how even the most elderly residents of these Pennine valley hamlets can take the most severe gradients in their stride, while we much younger 'flat-landers' seem to puff and blow along.

A compass reading should indicate that our route through Mossley is an easterly one, and so it should remain until meeting the junction with the B6175 and its small chapel set in the trees. A right turn here soon brings us to the cart-width Roman road branching to the left and the route to Buckton Castle. Micklehurst Cricket Club's sign shows the way, the club-house itself being directly opposite to the outline of the castle, clearly

visible in the pasture below the moor. Buckton Castle is a pre-Roman camp between the camps of Castleshaw, near Denshaw and Melandra, Derbyshire. Like so many so-called Roman camps and roads indicated on the OS map, Buckton Castle was of British origin, its rightful occupants being ousted by Roman invaders. Today, cattle graze and lapwings nest on the castle's grassy outline.

We pursue the Roman road into the hamlet of Carrbrook, where two rows of fine terraced houses are announced as, 'Oak Bank' and 'Thorn Bank'. This is the beginnings of Buckton Vale. Continuing through Carrbrook, we pass on our left Carrbrook Garage, which is well indicated, until we meet the first of two footpaths leading to the uplands, via Slatepit Moor. Save for sheep-tracks, the tops hereabouts are devoid of footpaths, and progress is a struggle through calf-deep heather, which rules out shorts as suitable attire.

Seen from the tops, Buckton Vale is a beautiful sight to behold, well wooded with oaks and hawthorns and fed by Carr Brook once the reservoir has secured its needs; several miles away to the west we see the outline of a huge horse, carved into a sandstone hillside. The climb to the heathery heights above Buckton Vale is short but very steep, skirting old disused quarry workings, now under the control of nature rather than the delph-man, and much better for that. In Spring and early Summer, the moorland sky here ripples with the songs of countless skylarks, the north-erners' nightingale, and the uncanny 'go back' call of the red grouse can be heard on the wind. This distinctive

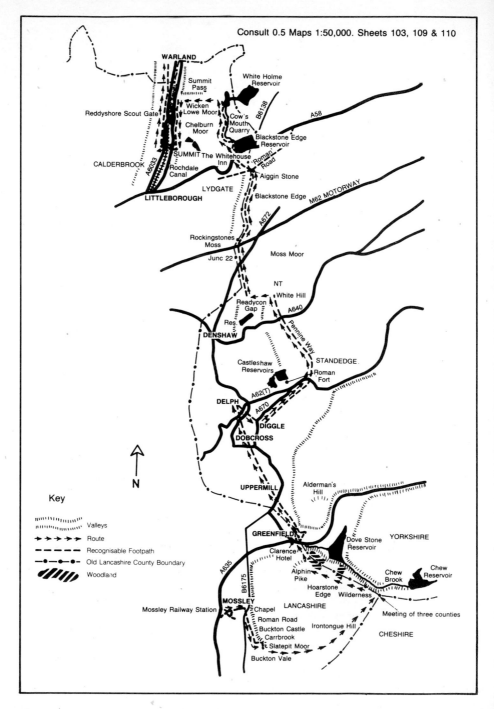

Consult 0.5 Maps 1:50,000. Sheets 103, 109 & 110

WARLAND

White Holme Reservoir

Summit Pass

Wicken Lowe Moor

Reddyshore Scout Gate

Chelburn Moor

Cow's Mouth Quarry

B6138

A58

Blackstone Edge Reservoir

CALDERBROOK

A6033

SUMMIT The Whitehouse Inn

Rochdale Canal

Roman Road

LITTLEBOROUGH

Aiggin Stone

LYDGATE

Blackstone Edge

M62 MOTORWAY

A672

Rockingstones Moss

Junc 22

Moss Moor

NT

White Hill

Readycon Gap

A640

Res.

Pennine Way

DENSHAW

Castleshaw Reservoirs

STANDEDGE

Roman Fort

A62(T)

DELPH

A670

DIGGLE

DOBCROSS

N

UPPERMILL

Alderman's Hill

GREENFIELD

Dove Stone Reservoir

YORKSHIRE

Key

Clarence Hotel

Chew Brook

Chew Reservoir

A635

Alphin Pike

Hoarstone Edge   Wilderness

B6175

Meeting of three counties

MOSSLEY

LANCASHIRE

Mossley Railway Station

Chapel

Roman Road

Buckton Castle

Irontongue Hill

CHESHIRE

Carrbrook

Slatepit Moor

Buckton Vale

Valleys

Route

Recognisable Footpath

Old Lancashire County Boundary

Woodland

10

Left: A tranquil view of Mossley, where our walk around the old Lancashire County boundary began. Terraced houses built using local stone are a common sight in many parts of Lancashire. Smoke from industry blackened such buildings in past years, but in more recent times they have been transformed by cleaning and renovation.

cry has made many a moorland rambler search the moor for an unwelcoming landowner, before realising who owned the voice!
Hoarstone Edge and Wilderness lie to the east of Buckton Vale; a few yards to the south the old Lancashire county boundary accompanies us.

To cross desolate Irontongue Hill is to cross a uniformity of peat-hags, moor-grass, cotton-sedge, heather and many peaty cloughs, of which the first-named are wide, deep and very slimy, and must be forded. Much of this area is also completely devoid of vegetation, the slopes made bare by too-frequent rains which flush any settled seeds away, leaving a vast sea of brown peat. One dreads to think what the outcome would be if a sudden downpour occurred, as it so often does in these Pennines, forcing the walker to cross a mile or so of this terrain in quagmire conditions, when it would undoubtedly attempt to engulf a person with every stride taken. On this particular day, however, a drying south-easterly wind dictates that clouds of peat dust are the order of the day.

The OS map indicates that the great rift in the moor to the north is the beginnings of Carr Brook, whilst to the north-east the horizon is dominated by Hoarstone Edge and Wilderness. Gathering clouds and a strong south-easterly wind which buffets the body are common on a Wilderness outing during the summer months, and for those in tune with solitary walks on the wild side there can be few better places than this. Heather and mixed cotton-sedge now replace the barren landscape of Irontongue Hill. This is a fine grouse moor, the young grouse when in flight resembling tennis balls with wings, and always accompanied by their much larger parents. It is here where the golden plover chooses to nest, a bird with which I am more familiar during winter months on the flat, lowland pastures of home, when its plumage is drab in comparison to its golden summer dress. Striking when at rest, swift and graceful when in flight, the golden plover breeds only on the wildest of moorlands.

The place-name *hoarstone* means ancient boundarystone, and this is what Hoarstone Edge represents. It separates Lancashire from Yorkshire, and to accomplish this plummets down some 500 feet into the bowels

11

Left: Buckton Vale, viewed from the hill-tops above the hamlet of Carrbrook, near Mossley. A marvellous spectacle.

of Chew Valley - a very impressive piece of natural architecture. As the whole area is a wilderness, Wilderness itself is rather difficult to distinguish, although it traditionally marks the spot where the old county boundaries of Lancashire, Cheshire and Yorkshire meet. Pennine traveller and author of the 1950s, Herbert C. Collins, refers to Wilderness and this area in general as: "a more suitable meeting place for Macbeth's three witches than three counties", which is a brief but apt description. There is always a wind to 'cut a whistle' in the moorgrass here, and I have yet to witness Chew Valley in mist-free conditions at Hoarstone Edge.

Looking into three counties from here, we see Yorkshire's Chew Reservoir, one misty mile away to the east, and built at the beginning of the First World War on the spa of Chew Well House, whose reputed healing waters attracted the unfortunate sick from far and wide. At 1,600 feet above sea level, Chew Reservoir can claim to be the highest reservoir in England. Just four miles to the north-east, although not visible on most occasions, Cheshire belies its reputation as a flat, arable county by rising to a dizzy 1,900 feet summit at Black Hill. It is, however, Lancashire which possesses the ancient legend of these moors. The old county boundary slowly descends at this point to the stone-built cairn of Alphin Pike, care-

Below: A jagged reminder of the last Ice Age, Hoarstone Edge marks the ancient boundary between Lancashire & Yorkshire. Chew Valley lies beyond the ancient rocks.

fully following the edge by way of rocky ramparts and rock-strewn moor-grass, which will make the wearer of sturdy boots count his blessings and the plimsolled walker count his blisters! This two-miles walk to Alphin Pike recalls the best of Lancashire folklore.

Alphin Pike is so-named in memory of a fight to the death that legend assures us took place here. This man-to-man conflict is said to have been fought by two massive giants of the moors hereabouts, Alphin and Alderman, the latter giant being represented by Alderman's Hill across the valley to the north. Legend records that both giants sought the charms of the beautiful shepherdess Rimmon, who would leave her leafy dell near Holme Moss, to bathe in unashamed nakedness in the stream of the clough that now bears her name. Her beauty and female finesse eventually attracted Alphin, the giant she desired, and they locked, so the story goes, in a passionate embrace on the summit of Alphin Pike. Meanwhile, Alderman, who was patrolling the tops of his domain, caught a glimpse of the entwined lovers and leapt headlong into a jealous rage, picking up and flinging a huge boulder at Alphin from across the valley. The primitive legend explains that in the following minutes Chew Valley was cast into darkness by the number of airborne boulders passing from one hill to the other until, finally, Alphin crumbled beneath a death-blow by Alderman.

Below: Pots and Pans Hill (left) and Alderman's Hill (right), Greenfield. According to local legend, a fatal duel between giants occurred here, the legacy of which are the boulder-strewn hillsides.

Alderman then crossed the valley to claim his prize of the desirable Rimmon, but the shepherdess was grief-stricken at the death of Alphin, who lay motionless on the valley floor. According to legend, Rimmon chose death rather than Alderman, and she cast herself from Alphin Pike to join her lover in eternity, leaving Alderman to roam the moors alone. He was never seen again.

The evidence of this duel to the death is the boulder-strewn valley flanks. Some of the boulders attain huge proportions, and to our ancestors they were believed to have been thrown by beings of immense size and strength. What other explanation can there be to a primitive race which knows nothing of terminal or lateral moraines from a distant Ice Age?

And so we walk down into the valley, pursuing the county boundary into Greenfield. To prevent trespassing on the Stalybridge Estates private grouse moor, the route down to Greenfield needs to be careful and precise. Standing at Alphin Pike's cairn, consult the compass, taking a north-easterly direction and thus keep within the confines of the Peak District National Park boundary. A conifer plantation in the valley marks the whereabouts of several footpaths into Greenfield, where the thirsty walker can take pleasure in a cool pint of ale at the nearest inn, the 'Clarence Hotel', on the corner of Chew Valley Road.

It is in the area's rugged hills and cloughs that much sheep-worrying has, over the years, given cause for concern amongst farmers. It isn't just the actual sheep-worrying that disturbs everyone, although this in itself is distressing enough, as the identity of the killer. Many sightings of a large puma-like creature have been reported to the police (the last sighting being in August, 1984), who retaliate with a force of marksmen to scour the moors in a thus-far vain attempt to unearth the elusive carnivore. The creature is said to be black, or dark in colour, of similar size and shape to a puma, and runs away at high speed when spotted, which is very reassuring to say the least!

Reports of similar 'large cat' sightings throughout the length and breadth of the country prompted BBC Television's *Tomorrows World* team to launch an investigation into this mystery in 1986. Using the latest technology in genetic identification, and actually catching what they believe to be one of these animals (not, it must be stressed, in our area!) the *Tomorrows World* team concluded that the animals are cats, a cross between the domestic black cat and the ferocious Scottish wildcat, which are now beginning to disperse southwards. However interesting this may be, nothing was found on the Lancashire moors, and the mystery remains unsolved.

Whilst on the subject of rare animals, it was whilst resting in the Greenfield uplands on one occasion that I was joined by a fell-runner, who told me about a sighting of three Arctic hares here during the winter of 1985/86. Being snow-white in winter, the Arctic hare changes colour with the seasons as a means of camouflage, and this sighting must surely have been a glimpse of Lancashire's rarest mammal.

At Greenfield, the old Lancashire county boundary neglects to follow what is an obvious northerly course or definement, the River Tame, preferring instead to visit the outskirts of Oldham. From Oldham the boundary turns northwards to almost meet the source of the River Tame, near Denshaw. This has provoked much comment and concern over the years from Lancastrians, who believe that the boundary should have pursued a course across the hilltops, following the edges by way of Standedge and on to the existing county line at Blackstone Edge. As it stands, the district of Saddleworth is in Yorkshire, even though its population have their roots in Rochdale and speak with a Lancashire dialect! Such are the oddities of life in the border country.

Until 1986, walkers were permitted to cross privately-owned Saddleworth Moor, a route through moorland bearing the ravages of the last Ice Age, with valleys of glacial moraine and spectacular standing stones. This walk met with the famous Pennine Way, where the 'Way' crosses the A635 at White Moss, to approach Standedge. Unfortunately, someone chose irresponsibility rather than common sense and climbed the

standing stones, a formidable task which they thought justified having their nick-names daubed in white paint on the summits. Since then, permission to cross Saddleworth Moor has been withdrawn by the landowner. For our part, we do not wish to pursue the old county boundary to the somewhat traffic-torn outskirts of Oldham, so we will take the route skirting the westerly boundary of the Peak District National Park to Standedge, which runs parallel to the River Tame, and is a pleasant walk.

From the 'Clarence Hotel', Greenfield, cross Chew Valley Road to pursue the wooded lane directly opposite, keeping hard by the church

Below: The standing stones on Saddleworth Moor, which command a breathtaking view. Note paint daubed on the rocks - a blemish on the landscape caused by thoughtless vandals.

wall. This is the A635. Take the first lane on your left after the church and follow the sign for Uppermill. From here, you can choose your own village-to- village walk to Standedge, taking in hamlets with rollicking names such as Dobcross, Delph and Diggle (all very popular tourist attractions in the summer months) which are well sign-posted and containing the best in country taverns, craft shops and their like. This is the district of Saddleworth, where old traditions are strictly adhered to, and used to supplement the diminiished incomes resulting from the death of 'King Cotton.' Lancashire's once-thriving cotton hamlets were pioneers in this trade, and they are setting an example once again, although this time on the tourist trail!

If your visit happens to be a summer Sunday afternoon and you are making for Uppermill, there will be little need of visual guidance from sign-posts, for a more prominent guide will be the sound of crisp cornets and thundering tubas from the brass band playing in the park. You will find this to be a packed venue, with all park benches taken, and where the silence from listeners during the music tells you that Lancashire's border country still delights in the solid sound of brass. Children more in tune with trout rather than trombones find that the neighbouring River Tame offers its bounty to those with even the most modest equipment. I once saw a small boy fishing here with make-shift tackle of a freshly-cut length of willow, a piece of cotton and a bent pin; his float was a match stick. Using worms dug from the bank as bait, out came fish up to four inches in length, one after another and each one bringing a smile to his face that no birthday present could ever hope to match. "They're dace, aren't they?"

I said, without knowing that I was putting a damper on his enthusiasm. "They're not dace", he said, rather defiantly. "They're trout, and if you don't believe me you can go and ask my dad, 'cos he's an expert on fish." We'll give his dad the benefit of the doubt.

Stone and yet more stone was used to build Saddleworth, quarried from the gaunt gritstone hills adjoining its back garden. Cleaned to its natural grey/brown colour, dressed gritstone bears little resemblance to the black, soot-stained outcrops to which we have become accustomed. So far as these soot-stained rocks are concerned, only a combination of the present smoke-free atmosphere and a great deal of weathering will enable them to present a cleaner face to the world as the years pass. Saddleworth Chapel was built using local stone in the 13th century by William de Stapleton, Lord of the Manor, although Saddleworth's present church , also of local stone,is of 19th century origin. Rushbearing is another tradition here, stemming from the days when rushes were laid on the church floor to keep warm the feet of the congregation. 1821 marks the last year that this took place, although the rushbearing traditionhas progressed with the times and is still staged to herald the beginning of important 'events' in the Saddleworth calendar.

Uppermill's main road is the A670 to Diggle, which meets with the A6052 Delph Road at Dobcross, giving a choice of three villages within one square mile. Delph was the home of the late Ammon Wrigley, whose books about these Pennines and their people are now much sought after by those with a feeling for these hills. He tells how his village and its immediate environs were once pestered by witches or boggarts,

Left: Saddleworth Church and the Church Inn, pictured on Rush-bearing Day (give date), still a local festival of great popularity. The church was built using locally quarried gritstone.

which for those unfamiliar with Lancashire lore, are ghosts or apparitions. Who wouldn't feel a little uneasy about rambling the moors hereabouts with boggarts, 'as big as a cart track and looking like a wool-sack with flaming eyes' to contend with? It is also said that horses can see boggarts whereas human beings cannot, and that therein lies the explanation as to why a horse may suddenly stampede or 'take boggarts' in otherwise calm conditions. Boggarts such as The Delph Hill End Baker, Old Delph Will, The Griffin Factory Marr, The New Tame Fiend, The Slackcote Thrasher and the Grange Bump, lead one to suspect that Delphonians of old seldom left their homes after 6.00 pm, especially on dark, winter nights!

Witches were said to harass the farmers by milking their cows dry whilst they slept. Consequently, cattle grazed the pastures with bible verses attatched to their horns and the parson was often asked to conduct 'witch laying' services. The packhorse men attempted to suppress the problem by hewing a hole through the upper half of a waystone sited at a known 'infested' area along their route, which hopefully diluted the potent magic of witches and quelled the burning antics of boggarts. The idea of the holed waystone was a consequence of the belief that boggarts depended upon a surprise attack, lurking in the shadows or behind a waystone in a slimmed-down form to suddenly emerge like the fires of hell. A holed waystone permitted a likely victim to see beforehand whether or not anything resembling 'a wool-sack with flaming eyes' was waiting to pounce. It was also believed that witches and boggarts could not cross open water, which is why we still see unbridged Pennine streams flowing across pack-horse tracks and other lonely moorland byways.

Delph is a hamlet with much of yesteryear still evident, the authorities preferring to construct a completely new village with the appropriate name of New Delph. The A6052 bisects the original village, twisting and turning between well-wooded gardens fronting old houses, and its tall mill, at an acute bend. With the blink of an eye the hamlet is behind you. The builders of old constructed the handloom weavers' cottages hard by the uplift of northern moor with its packhorse tracks, so that the traveller on the east- west course of the A6052 is unaware of their presence. Thus, today's motorist unfortunately sees very little of this spendidly preserved village.

An hourly Sunday bus service, introduced in 1986 and named 'Pennine Edge', runs from Bury to Holmfirth, operating from the beginning of May until the beginning of October. The route is: Bury, Heywood, Rochdale, Hollingworth Lake Country Park, Milnrow, Newhey, Denshaw, Delph, Dobcross, Uppermill, Greenfield and across the old county boundary to Yorkshire's Holmfirth, via the remote high moorland A635, known locally as the Isles of Skye Road. For those with time for sightseeing, the trip from Greenfield to Holmfirth was around 60p in early 1988. This is a new type of bus service, where the passenger can board or alight anywhere along the route without having to seek a recognised bus stop - just 'stick out your hand' from the roadside when you want to board, or tell the driver when you want to alight. Holmfirth (local dialect pronounces it Holmfrith) is of course, the location of the TV comedy series *Last of the Summer Wine,* and the journey to the hamlet offers spectacular views of Saddleworth Moors. You will also be in compatible company - the service is well used by walkers.

Your last hamlet to visit should be Diggle, from where a conglomeration of footpaths lead to Standedge, where the Pennine Way crosses the A62 (T) road. From the relative comfort of village life, we now return to wilder terrain once more, where gritstone outcrops are weathered into wierd and wonderful shapes, pot-holed and wrinkled and looking more like the tough hide of a dinosaur than the material of which many local buildings are made. Standedge is a notorious winter 'black spot', and is reagularly mentioned in winter weather reports on local radio, for the A62 (T) road is frequently blocked, its vehicles being hopelessly trapped in snow, often roof-deep. It's all good photographic material for local newspapers too, who have been sending photographers to Standedge year after year since the camera was invented, to picture the scene of man's struggle with the elements.

Below us, to the west, is Castleshaw Reservoirs and Castleshaw Roman Camp. Constructed in AD 79 by Julius Agricola (although believed to occupy the site of an earlier British camp) a feature of this Roman garrison has been the discovery of a central heating arrangement, or hypocaust; this was an underground chamber in which a fire was made, and heat dispersed to the men's quarters via a system of flues. Once again, there is little to see today of this camp save for its outline, which reveals that a small camp was constructed within a larger settlement some three acres in extent. Some 1st century pottery, Roman coins and a tile with the lettering COH 111 BRE were discovered here. Tools and flints of Neolithic man have also been found in these hills, a significant find being a stone celt (chisel) unearthed during the construction of Castleshaw Reservoir. Greater Manchester Archaeological Unit are at present excavating Castleshaw Roman Fort, which they claim to be one of the finest turf and timber forts in the north of England.

Looming above and to the northwest of Castleshaw Reservoirs is the cairn of Broadhead Noddle, below which a roughly stoned packhorse track leads to Denshaw. Here is a small hamlet with many inns - there seems to be one on every corner - and every one is amply tested during the summer months by large numbers of Pennine Way walkers.

We are now approaching Readycon Gap, where we encounter walking country which demands dogged determination and sturdy legs to circumvent its body traps of ankle-twisting tussocks and hidden bog-holes. We are also approaching the old Lancashire county boundary, which follows the course of the Pennine Way for a few miles from this point. Undefined and difficult to locate through centuries-old sheep tracks branching in all directions, the Pennine Way cuts a dog's leg from the National Trust area at White Hill, first running west for half-a-mile via a triangulation pillar into Readycon Gap, and then northwards to pick up the posts marking the 'Way' across Moss Moor. The walker must consult his compass.

Cloud-wrack is a climatic menace in Readycon Gap, rolling down the hillside at the drop of a hat to transform a bright, clear day into one of blanket fog in a matter of minutes. I have been here when knee-deep mist has made safe walking impossible, even though above waist level visibility has been fine. A map, compass and hard weather attire are a necessity in this part of the world, no matter the season, and the local warning that, 'we can have four seasons here in one day', is not exaggerated; it is a sound warning to heed.

Some people believe that a Roman road lies hidden beneath the turf of Readycon Gap, a connection between the Roman road at Blackstone Edge and the Roman fort at Castleshaw, which we passed earlier. It takes little imagination to picture soldiers of the Sixth Legion of Rome, once governors of this area, patrolling this wild

landscape, or even our Neolithic ancestors, shaping stone implements around a fire. There is a powerful sense of long ago here, a primeval air of a land just abandoned by primitive man, held in suspended animation. The knowledge that a carnivorous beast (remember the wild cats?) stalks these hills adds to this threatening, mysterious atmosphere. Likewise the curlew's haunting cry, and hares seen in silhouette at dusk against a fire red sky.

Deeply rutted and obviously well-trodden the Pennine Way marches across Moss Moor, and for those in harmony with nature this is a credible stretch of countryside. In the correct season it is a tableland of flowering cotton-grass, and again is the home of the golden plover, a bird which is becoming increasingly rare. This moorland is used increasingly for recreation by the neighbouring densely populated regions of Greater Manchester. Please treat birds - and indeed all wildlife - with respect. As with the curlew, the wild moors just wouldn't be the same without birds like the golden plover.

We cross the A672 at appropriately named Windy Hill to meet the Pennine Way footbridge spanning the M62 Trans-Pennine motorway, the highest footbridge across a motorway in the country. This is the notorious Junction 22 or Rockingstones Moss, 1,500 feet above sea level and with a climate to match. Constructing this motorway proved to be the most difficult construction project this country has to date undertaken. Mining subsidence, the Pendleton and Tunshill Faults (subterranean instability) wind speeds of up to 120 mph, 60 inches of rainfall in some years, sometimes snow for six months of the year and 20 feet of peat deposited on a bed of gritstone, were some of the engineering headaches to be overcome. One engineer is quoted as saying that, on warm days, so much moisture rose out of the peat that it appeared as if it was raining upwards!

Needless to say, motorway pile-ups are an annual occurrence, the last one as I write being on January 14 1987, when 660 vehicles and their drivers were stranded in blizzard conditions at junction 22 for 36 hours. "I was in the Arctic last year," remarked one wagon driver, "and conditions were no worse than this". A policeman explained: "The wind was so strong that it ripped both doors off our Rangerover and carried them away like pieces of paper". The power of the elements indeed.

Crossing the motorway footbridge brings us to moorland of the bleakest kind, undulating and boulder strewn, all but devoid of life save for the outbursts of occasional meadow pipits. Hard-bitten and inhospitable accurately describes this terrain, a fitting location for a Dickensian-type script demanding a backdrop of impoverished. eerie moor. To the west, the back-bone of Rochdale's Rooley Moor dominates the landscape, 1,555 feet above sea level and boasting one of England's highest metalled roads. From this vantage point, Lancashire appears to be a wilderness of rolling hills, with little indication that the enormous Greater Manchester population is going about its business in the valleys below. Yorkshire lies to the east of our route, and offers the walker much in scenic value with acre upon acre of yawning moor melting into the misty distance.

Moor, mire and moraine: Blackstone Edge announces its beginnings. Gigantic boulders litter the landscape, some perching precariously one on top of the other along the 1,550 contour edge, and they are at their most impressive at Robin Hood's Bed, where a precipitous gritstone

massif towers above the tiny hamlet of Lydgate. Here too is what our ancestors believed to be the work of an enraged giant, who tore down the walls of his own castle, flinging the masonary far and wide. This is the formidable barrier between Lancashire and Yorkshire, the thorn in the side of early travellers such as William Camden, who appealed for help from the Almighty before crossing this great divide: "I must now turn the course of my journey another way, unto the rest of the Brigantes, who are planted on the farther side of the Hilles toward the Irish Sea; and first into Lancashire which I go unto (God speed me well) after a sort somewhat against my will". This was Tudor period Blackstone Edge, as seen from Yorkshire.

In 1698, Celia Fiennes, a much-travelled lady of the time, referred to Blackstone Edge as: "a most dismal, high precipice with mists and raines almost perpetually", while in August 1724, novelist and politician Daniel Defoe was enduring a blinding snowstorm which was "cold acute and piercing".

The place-name Robin Hood is mentioned quite frequently in these Pennines and originates, according to several distinguished sources, from fact rather than fancy. The famous Robin Hood, so the story goes, was actually a Yorkshireman who died at Kirklees Priory, near Halifax. During the reign of King John, a large proportion of the landscape hereabouts is believed to have been clad with a forest (which has given rise to the Sherwood Forest aspect of the legend) which, as a result of the outlaw's heroism, had its more permanent or useful features named after him. Thus, we have ancient Robin Hood's Well. just eight miles away to the west at Helmshore, and Robin Hoods Rocks at Cragg Vale.

Above: The mysterious Roman Road, at Blackstone Edge: the original purpose of the grooved centre channel stones remains a mystery.

According to this version of the classic tale, the outlaw's links with Nottingham are wholly fictitious......

It is, however, the putative Roman road, now a National Monument, which ascends Blackstone Edge from Lygate on the Lancashire side to Yorkshire's Black Castle Clough that lures interest here. Who actually constructed this remarkable highway? Achieving in places a one in four gradient, the sixteen and half feet wide causey has a centre line of troughstones and is cambered with side gutters for drainage purposes. Obviously, the troughstones were put to some practical use other than simply channelling away excess water and suggestions have been forthcoming since the 17th century. These include theories as ambitious as transporting Danish war-ships over the

'Edge', to a more modest pack-sledge run. The former theory suggests that the troughstones were worn into grooves, the latter that they were hewn in this fashion. Considering that Blackstone Edge is sometimes a blanket of snow for six months of the year, a facility to ease transportation during such conditions appears to be a logical precaution. A pack-sledge would be a sound alternative to wheeled transport during severe winter weather. The idea that ships were transported over the moor cannot be wholly dismissed however, for on the Yorkshire side of Blackstone Edge the road is known as Danes' Road rather than The Roman Road.

There is little doubt that the road existed during the Roman occupation of the area, or that the Romans used it. The unearthing of a silver arm of a Statue of Victory dedicated to Valarius Rufus of the Sixth Legion substantiates this fact. But the question remains: did the Romans build the road, or did they merely make use of an established highway?

At the sumit of the so-called Roman road stands a wedge-shaped gritstone monolith, 7ft high and inscribed with a Latin cross and the initials 'IT'. Known as Aiggin Stone, the derivation of which is vague, it is believed to mark the road's highest point. Here is a good spot to ponder the past whilst enjoying the silence, interrupted only by the moaning wind in the moorgrass, which complements Aiggin Stone's sinister surroundings to give more than a little atmospheric substance to the claim that a pack of spectre hounds haunts eerie Blackstone Edge. Many a lost and lonely mill-girl has explained with bated breath how these translucent canines routed her to safety, after which they dissolved into the dank moor once their good deed was done!

Many hours can be whiled away at Blackstone Edge, seeking out the initials hewn into the boulders by Pennine travellers of distant days. Hargreaves Tattersall, Newhaven, America, 1891, is one inscription carried by a rock holding a prominent position above Robin Hood's Bed. It is cut with the craftmanship of a mason into a gritstone massif. Search for a longer period and over a wider area to discover 16th and 17th century initials.

One has to be in tune with stark and sombre surroundings to fully appreciate Blackstone Edge. It isn't the type of countryside to attract the naturalist, nor can it be described as beautiful in the accepted sense of the word. "Magnificent, but never beautiful", said one visitor. Backpackers know that March and April visits can result in the skin being flayed from the face through gale-blown gritstone chips. "It's like someone continually rubbing your face with sandpaper", remarked one backpacker who had suffered the experience. "It stings and eventually draws blood if you're in it for too long".

What is fascinating about Blackstone Edge is that it has never changed with the passing of time. Man has had little influence here save for his wayfaring activities, which have worn the Pennine Way route down to a depth of two feet in places - and this is solid gritstone! It isn't so much due to modern Pennine Way walkers that path erosion is so pronounced here, rather the length of time this route has been in use. Today's walkers follow the very same route as that chosen by Stone-Age man, and many a Roman soldier has lamented at leaving his much warmer, native country whilst struggling along this path in a Blackstone Edge blizzard. It is a place where a 16th century map still compares with its present-day equivalent, and where descriptions by 14th and 15th century luminaries still hold true. Here is a primitive landscape which is simultaneously rough, rugged and rigorous, and with a riotous climate that isn't expected at a modest 1,500 feet contour. Daniel Defoe referred to Blackstone Edge as 'England's Andes', and he rated this range of hills way ahead of the Lake District in the climatic catastrophe stakes. Blackstone Edge is still as the last Ice Age left it.

At the time of writing, the climatic ravages of 2,000 years on the Roman Road was due to be repaired, certainly on the lower reaches, where natural undermining has caused problems. Here also is an ash car-park, from where visitors with sturdy legs and lungs can tread the stone sets to the summit, a one mile walk which will even test the respiration of an athlete!

Down in the valley to the south-west is some of the coldest water in England, so cold in fact that Captain Webb (famous from the matches named after him!) believed it to be the perfect stretch of training water for his cross-Channel swimming attempts. This is Littleborough's Hollingworth Lake, now said to be the most popular country park in the country, and constructed in 1801 as a compensation reservoir to keep the Rockdale Canal topped-up - in its heyday the Canal took one million gallons of Hollingworth Lake water per day to keep its barges on the move. To the Victorians, however, the lake was better known as a place of steam-boat rides, dancing, general merry-making and much drunkenness, with fine hotels and cafes along its shoreline. Today, you will find the Fish Inn, formerly known as the Fisherman's Inn, and the Beach Tavern, together with lakeside amuse-ments and refreshment stalls. You are not likely to find many swimmers, however, not even on the warmest of days. "Many have tried to swim the length of the lake", I was informed, "and many have had to give up before reaching half way. The water is just too cold..."

One person who, like Captain Webb, finds Hollingworth Lake cold enough for his training is 38 years old Cliff Kelleher, a long distance swimmer from my home town of Leigh. Chosen to represent Great Britain in 1984 and 1985 in a three miles canal swim in Belgium, swimming instructor Cliff was a member of the Howe Bridge Cross Channel Relay Team in 1986, when they took the world record for the event. Cliff's more usual swims, however, range from one mile to ten

Below: Leigh long-distance swimmer Cliff Kelleher, training in Hollingworth Lake, said to be the coldest water in England.

miles, with the lengths of Windermere and Coniston Water being just two of the 14 long distance swims he accomplished during 1987. Since 1979 when he began long-distance swimming, he has competed in 65 events. Now with five records for outdoor swimming under his belt, not to mention a lounge full of trophies, his sights are firmly set on swimming two lengths of Lake Windermere and a solo cross-Channel breast-stroke attempt. "Two lengths of Lake Windermere are 21 miles" explained Cliff, "which means that I will be in the water for15 hours or more. I'll attempt it if I feel fit enough following the 1987 Channel relay swim".

Cliff explained that the problem with swimming the English Channel is one of finance rather than the swim itself. "It costs about £600 for the hire of a boat", he said "and you still have to pay the whole fee if you only manage to swim 100 yards from the shore". He continued: "Not so many have done the English Channel by breast-stroke, although a girl from Bury has accomplished the swim. I'd really like to have a go at this before I retire..."

"What are you going to do when you retire from swimming?" I asked him.

"I think I'll walk the Pennine Way to start with", he replied.

I left Cliff to his Hollingworth Lake training session and wished him good luck in his future swims. His body was a salmon-pink colour. "That tells you how cold Hollingworth Lake is", he said as I sought the footpath running north-east by the Fish Inn, bound for the hamlet of Lydgate.

From Hollingworth Lake to Lydgate occupies approximately a mile-and -a-half of lowland moor walking. At Lydgate you would have found until 1987 'The Lydgate', a country inn which provided Saturday night disco entertainment before fire gutted its interior. En route to the inn, on the tarmac road through the hamlet, you would have also found two sheep-dogs on long leashes with a kennel for each dog at the roadside. Their duty was to prevent sheep from wandering down the road to Littleborough. This was a sensible precaution, although the sheep-dogs in their enthusiasm also attempted to prevent people from wandering down the road; eventually a fell-runner was bitten, since when the dogs have been removed. This I find odd, as a sharp word of check soon had the two sheep-dogs back in their kennels.

Until 1943, 'The Lydgate' was known as 'The Gate Inn', and rather than a disco it had for entertainment egg-judging and eating competitions, the prize-winning eggs being chosen for their size and levelness. Following the egg-judging, all the eggs were cracked into pints of ale, sometimes as many as eight eggs to one pint for those with the stomach for it, and a grand evening was had by all!

Littleborough's Emily Rushton remembers with affection the happy days of 'The Gate Inn.' Emily, with her husband Isaac, was licencee of the inn from 1934 until 1944, and recalls: "It was a good house, and there was always something going on of a Saturday night. We also used to brew tea for hikers, as we called 'em in them days". Above the door of' The Gate Inn' was a wayfarer's welcome, informing one and all that:

"This Gate hangs well, and hinders none. Refresh and pay, and travel on".

"There was a tap-room for t' farmers and a parlour for t' courting couples", explained Emily, who is now in her 'eighties, "and we used to sell Ramsdens and John Smiths ales and Whitakers whisky". When the inn closed for modernisation and resumed trading under its new name of The Lydgate, Emily was called upon to crown the event by pumping the first pint, although whether or not following this recent fire she will once again be required to perform a similar ceremony is a matter that hangs in the balance. At the time of writing, this 18th century pack-horse pub that dwells in a dip is on offer to the highest bidder. Let us hope that it retains its life-long role as an inn...

Two miles to the north-east of Lydgate in the valley taking the A58 Rochdale to Halifax road is the splendid 'Coach and Horses Inn', now renamed 'The Whitehouse Inn.' Situated hard by Blackstone Edge Reservoir and scraping into Lancashire by the skin of its teeth, the inn is directly on the Pennine Way close to the now disused old coaching road. The inn once served the needs for Perseverence, High Flyer, Commerce, The Duke of Leeds and others, all stagecoaches which picked up passengers on the old coaching road at Littleborough's 'Rake Inn,' which is an old pack-horse pub with a resident and frequently-observed cavalier ghost and its still extant stone horse-trough brimming with crystal-clear brook water. From here, the stagecoaches sped to the toll house at the hamlet of Lydgate, now the home of farmer William Shaw, and on to Halifax via the 'Coach and Horses' Inn. Today, the inn serves the needs of Pennine Way backpackers and is affectionately known as 'The Watering Hole.' Needless to say that the route to the inn is well trodden!

I held a lengthy discussion with 75 years old William Shaw, of the old toll house, now known as Rough Farm, who, since August 1987, has been living in a Grade One listed building and who has farmed these bleak Pennine uplands for more than 55 years. "I bowt th'old toll house in 1951 for £1,200 when nobody thowt it was th'owld toll house", William informed me, "and ney I gets offers of over £60,000 for it, but I can't be bothered movin' at my age".

Adjoining the early 18th century toll house is a single-roomed outbuilding, now used as a storeroom, still with its single, small-mullioned window set in the hammer-dressed stonework of the rear wall, where stagecoach passengers would alight to pay their fares. The old toll house has changed little since construction, and retains its original quoins (or corner stones) and mullioned windows.

As might be expected, the old toll house is reputedly haunted: "I once saw a grey-faced owld mon standin' at foot o' mi bed", explained William, "and I'm not coddin' thi. I nudged wife for t' wake her up, but he disappeared afore she could see him".

"Who was he?" I asked. "The Grim Reaper?"

"I don't know who he was", William replied, "but wife was dead within a fortnit'". He also told me how, as a child, the story surrounding Robin Hood in these Pennines was taught in school. "They towld us at school that Robin Hood was in hidin' at a place near th'arches in Littlebor', and that king's men flushed 'im out so as he made for Robin Hood's Bed o'er theer by Blackstone Edge. They used tak' us from school for t' show us spot behind a fanlight weer they flushed 'im, but ney they've pulled buildin' down".

During my time spent with William Shaw he was concerned about the fish children were catching in one of his two lodges behind his home.

Facing page: William Shaw, of Rough Farm, Blackstone Edge. Was it the 'Grim Reaper' he saw one night, standing at the foot of his bed?

"Every time they catch a fair sized un they gi' it me for t' eat", he said, "and I keeps cloddin' 'em at back o' t' fire. Yon' kids must think I'm eatin' six o' these a day, although I can't say as I like look o' yon' rough-backed-uns for eatin'". Those 'rough-backed-uns' were perch weighing in at around a pound-and-a-half, and I explained that when soaked overnight in salt-water and grilled, they were delicious. "Perch are they?" he said. "I won-dered what they were wi' havin' rough backs wi' stripes and a big spiney fin on their back for stingin' thi wi'. Anyway, I'll try yon' wi' some chips tomorrer neet". I sincerely hope William enjoyed his perch and chips, and I left him to the tune of what I assumed to be a canary singing in his front room. 'No. It's not a canary", he replied. "It's a parrot that sings alot..."

From Lydgate, which local dialect pronounces as Lydiate, the Pennine Way is re-located by pursuing the Roman Road to its summit, from where the Way ventures forth to skirt Blackstone Edge Reservoir, making an acute turn to the west from the 'Coach and Horses' inn, where you you will embark along a stoned track into more barren windeness of the type previously described. We trace the course of Regulating Drain, marked on the OS map, to Cow's Mouth Quarry, now disused and a practice precipice for budding moun-taineers, until a sign announces White Holme Reservoir. Here, the old Lancashire county boundary aban-dons the 1,200 feet contour Pennine Way to traverse the 900 feet dip of Wicken Lowe Moor, towards Summit Pass, which is a directly western approach.

Severe subterranean fires have undermined this stretch of moor, transforming what should be just one mile as the crow flies to Summit Pass,

into several miles as the snake crawls. Caution is required to avoid the pits of black peat-ash lying beneath a thin grass surface, the safe route being a stepping-stone approach across the glacial moraine. Even the usually sure-footed sheep have fallen victim to this hidden hazard and perished neck-deep in peat-ash. This route to Summit Pass should only be attempt-ed when the moor is free of mist, when the walker will find it a worth-while exercise.

Summit Pass comes as a sudden surprise, for Wicken Lowe Moor is discovered in reality to be 'Wicken high', terminating at a precipice that plunges 700 feet down the throat of the pass. Only a broken fence sepa-rates the walker from this fall to certain death, which amplifies my earlier warning that mist-free condi-tions should exist when you cross Wicken Lowe Moor.

Summit Village is situated on the A6033 Littleborough to Todmorden road, below Chelburn Moor, a hamlet of ribbon development that grew up with the coming of road, rail and canal communications here. From the Summit Pass viewpoint on Wicken Lowe Moor, take a southerly direction along the ridge of Chelburn Moor, which runs parallel with the Rochdale Canal in the valley. Slowly descending the path leads to the canal's Chelburn Locks, Lock-keeper's Cottage and bridge, from where a lane connects with the bridge to locate the A6033 and 'The Summit Inn.'

Packhorse causeys criss-cross this region in confusion. We are at the hub of a one-time thriving hand-loom weaving industry, which initiated tough, cash-conscious drovers to con-struct their own moorland routes to transport the weaves to merchants, thus avoiding costly turnpike charges and initiating new routes from village to village. Coal, iron-ore, and lime to sweeten the peaty, acid soils of the district were other commodities transported by pack-horse. The horses to do this work came from Galloway and were knows as Limegals, a very hardy, amiable breed which thought little of these far more temperate southerly climes. Traverse these moors during the freezing depths of winter, when a cutting east wind blows and you will soon realise what solid stuff the packhorse men were made of!

Our journey now takes us by one of the most famous of packhorse tracks to Warland. This is Reddsyhore Scout Gate, the first man-made communication through Summit Pass, and constructed, it is believed, along the line of an ancient Anglo-Saxon route which gave access to the then forested, game-inhabited flank of the Pass; today it connects Calderbrook's old Turnpike road with Todmorden, some five miles away. From the 'Summit Inn' cross the A6033 to the opposing footpath. Turn left (south) here, walking by shops and two chapels (on your left) until meeting (on your right) a narrow, steep and stepped footpath to Calderbrook. Take the path to turn right at Calderbrook, following the old metalled coaching road, which runs into Reddyshore Scout Gate.

The name Gate is frequently encountered in these Pennines, and means 'a road.' Likewise Scout, meaning a hill, rake meaning a steep incline, and shore meaning an edge. Thus Reddyshore South Gate is easy of interpretation: Reddy refers to a road once discoloured through iron-ore droppings being deposited during transportation, or the natural sandy colour of the rock, while shore, scout and gate explain that here is a road running along the edge of a hill.

From the heights of Reddyshore Scout Gate we see the Rochdale Canal unwinding towards Todmorden, although today it no longer accommodates, as it did in 1888, 50 barges a day, with a combined, loaded weight of a staggering 686,000 tons annually. On February 10 1805, the *Mayflower* sailed quietly down the canal on its journey from London to Liverpool Docks, where many people gathered to see her arrive as the first vessel to do so by inland navigation. Today the Rochdale Canal is a slumbersome waterway with underworked locks, the haunt of pleasure-boaters, anglers and towpath strollers. Just to the west of the canal is the A6033 and to the west of the road the Summit railway, whose tunnel was built in 1841 to forever remind us of George Stephenson's faith in his own engineering ability: "I will stake my character and my head if that tunnel ever give way so as to cause danger to the public passing through it. Taking it as a whole, I doubt there is such another piece of work in the world".

Stephenson's claim was put to the test in 1984, when a week-long blaze resulting from exploding petrol tankers failed to bring down the tunnel. "Here is a marvellous feat of engineering", said a British Rail spokesman. "They certainly knew how to build in those days". Stephenson would have been delighted!

Finally, above and to the west of Summit railway tunnel is our route, Reddyshore Scout Gate. Wide enough for a horse and cart and hewn by hand using hammer and wedge from the rocky flank of the Pass. Notice the huge gritstone boulders which have been hewn away to forge the route and the sections of original pavement. The actual date of con-

Facing page: Reddyshore Scout Gate packhorse track, the first man-made communications route through the Summit Pass, where boggarts once made mischief!

Above: The Rochdale canal unwinds through the Summit Pass, towards Walden. On the left of the canal is the A6033, beyond which is the Summit railway tunnel.

struction isn't known, although we do know that Reddyshore Scout Gate was well established as a trading route when the Calderbrook Turnpike road was completed in 1795.

Summit Pass still reveals the scars and lacerations inflicted upon it from past, intense quarrying carried out to provide raw materials necessary for construction of roads and railways, and the cost in aesthetic terms has been considerable. Chelburn Wood, Grove, Timbercliffe and Sladen Wood are now simply place-names to recall a once-sylvan Summit Pass, while some of the blasting debris along the flank of Reddyshore Scout Gate has

refused to submit to natural landscaping, and has retained instead its initial rock-strewn appearance , following the obviously enthusiastic endeavours of George Stephenson's dynamite men. Even amidst all of this chaos however, it is easy to peer into this huge natural fissure and picture its once unspoiled grandeur, or let your imagination take you back 200 years to 1788 when packhorse men followed the wilderness-like route to Todmorden. We are at Warland, where the old county boundary neglects the 'edges' to bite into the western moor to locate the tops...

OUR route now treads the splendid moorland pastures of Shore Moor, lush and green and tended in the first instance 1,000 years ago by Anglo-Saxon farmers. This is sheep country in the best sense, sometimes tall, tough and tussocky, sometimes cropped to the root-fibres by nibbling jaws, and sometimes strewn with gritstone slabs, which the last Ice Age laid down here to resemble a giant pack of fallen dominoes. Walking is pleasant where the gritstone base has permitted only a dusting of top-soil, thus preventing moor-grass invasion, which loves to get its roots deep in juicy, acid peat. In the sodden sumps and hollows it achieves ankle-twisting proportions with root tussocks two to feet high - the largest, toughest moor-grass roots I have ever encountered. The scientific name for this vigorous moor-claiming species is *Molinia caerulea,* from the Spanish botanist, *Molinia,* who first identified it. We know it as purple moor-grass, and as a species which flourishes when burned, it soon replaces heather on poorly-managed moors where burning is carried out either too frequently, or at the wrong time of the year. The Anglo-Saxons knew the grass as the raw material from which to make a coarse type of twine or rope. The grouse-shooter, on the other hand, knows that the arrival of this grass heralds the demise of his sport, for the red grouse disappear with the heather, their basic food.

Compass navigation along sheep tracks is the sensible course to take, maintaining a south-westerly direction until Watergrove Reservoir is sighted in the Wardle Valley on your left, from whence the route is a westerly one. In the correct season you will

be accompanied by several curlews, flush skylarks and meadow pipits - they will appear from almost beneath your feet as you walk. A healthy pasture moor such as this supports a healthy insect population, which in turn attracts an abundance of insect-eating birds; Springtime witnesses the jackdaw searching the cropped pastures for worms and land molluscs, although they are really here to mingle with the sheep, upon whose backs they strut, beaks feverishly probing the wool to root out their favourite delicacy, the 'ked', or sheep-tick. Some of the birds fly with wool trailing from their beaks, heading for Whitworth's St Bartholomews Church, in whose high and gargoyled tower they will build their nests.

The old county boundary now heads for the 1,340 feet summit of Crook Hill, on top of which is a hole, bored deep into the skull of the hill, which permitted access for just one very courageous and non-claustro-phobic miner. Down the hill's west-erly flank is the waste of those mining endeavours - tons and tons of piled-high shale. Old packhorse tracks radiate from the base of Crook Hill like the spokes of a wheel, centuries old, yet still displaying deep cart-tracks. We are in the once-prosper-ous Wardle Valley, whose community busied itself with coal mining and hand-loom weaving. Today, the 17th century farmsteads are tumbled and ruinous, many having been drowned when the valley was partly flooded to accommodate Watergrove Reservoir.

Down in the Kirklees Valley, to the south-west, is Greenmount Wild Bird Hospital, run by Irena Zalasiewicz, a lady of Polish origin who came to this country at the end of the Second

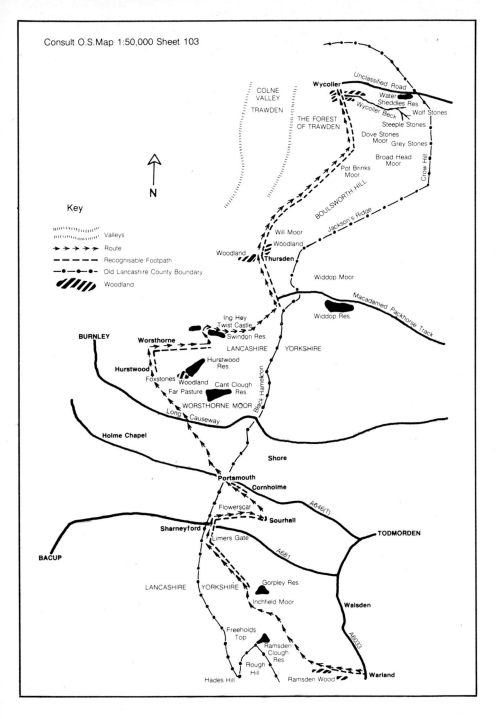

Consult O.S. Map 1:50,000 Sheet 103

COLNE VALLEY
TRAWDEN

THE FOREST OF TRAWDEN

N

Key

'''''''''''	Valleys
→ → → → →	Route
– – – – –	Recognisable Footpath
•—•—•—•	Old Lancashire County Boundary
◆◆◆◆	Woodland

Wycoller
Unclassified Road
Water Sheddles Res
Wycoller Beck
Wolf Stones
Steeple Stones
Dove Stones Moor
Grey Stones
Broad Head Moor
Crow Hill
Pot Brinks Moor
BOULSWORTH HILL
Jackson's Ridge
Will Moor
Woodland
Woodland
Thursden
Widdop Moor
Macadamed Packhorse Track
Widdop Res.
Ing Hey
Twist Castle
Swindon Res.
BURNLEY
Worsthorne
LANCASHIRE   YORKSHIRE
Hurstwood
Hurstwood Res.
Foxstones
Woodland
Cant Clough Res.
Far Pasture
Black Hameldon
WORSTHORNE MOOR
Long Causeway
Holme Chapel
Shore
Portsmouth
Cornholme
Flowerscar
Sourhall
A646(T)
Sharneyford
Limers Gate
A681
TODMORDEN
BACUP
LANCASHIRE   YORKSHIRE
Gorpley Res.
Inchfield Moor
Walsden
Freeholds Top
A6033
Ramsden Clough Res.
Rough Hill
Hades Hill
Ramsden Wood
Warland

Right: Irena Zalasiewicz, with one of several blind tawny owls in permanent care at the Green mount Wild Bird Hospital. "Rodents eat chemically-treated grain," she says," and the owls suffer eventual blindness by eating the poisoned rodents."

Facing page: Still in remarkably good repair, the Limers Gate packhorse track threads the moorland mist en route to Lancaster, close to Whitworth's Brown Wardle Hill. Imagine travelling this highway, by horse and cart, in a wild storm......

World War, when she was demobbed from the British Eighth Army Division. At the age of 16 years, Irena was taken from her native Poland by the Communist forces to suffer the hardships of a Russian labour camp, where she worked as a lumberjack in the one million square miles of forest close to the Arctic Circle, said to be the largest forest in the world. However, starvation, cold and disease began to take their toll, and Irena was transferred to the burial detail, sometimes burying as many as 60 bodies daily, including her parents. "The only thing that kept me going", she told me, "was the wildlife of the forest, especially the wild flowers which, in Spring, follow the receeding snow and ice in a display of colour that you couldn't imagine".

Eventually Irena and all other labour camp detainees were marched 1,000 miles across the Arctic Tundra to fight on the Russian Front. "How many we buried along the way I'll never know", she informed me. "It was difficult to understand how so much cruelty could exist amongst so much natural beauty". Irena's ordeal lasted

a full two years before liberation came, when her training as a nurse in the Polish ATS was recognised by the British 8th Army Division, who recruited her into their fighting force where she tended to the needs of the wounded until the end of the war.

Now, this tough little lady concentrates all her efforts on the welfare of wild birds, caring for the injured and sick of the natural world with the same dedication that brought her through her wartime ordeal. "I owe a great debt of gratitude to the natural world", Irena explained, "and caring for nature's casualties is my way of repayment".

From the humble beginnings of a small shed behind her house where she nursed a sparrow back to health, to today's splendid Greenmount Wild Bird Hospital in Kirklees Valley, which caters for all species of wild birds, Irena now runs a registered charity treating and releasing more than 500 birds each year. The land which the aviaries and hospital building occupy is leased to Irena at a peppercorn rent by Courtaulds Ltd, and operations are performed by vet-

erinary surgeons who donate their skills free of charge; Greenmount Wild Bird Hospital is one of only a handful in the country performing life-saving operations on wild birds.

During my visit, the hospital was treating herons, barn and tawny owls, a kingfisher and a Manx shearwater, to name but a few, and it provides a splendid opportunity for schoolchildren to study British wild birds at close quarters. Admission to Greenmount Wild Bird Hospital is free each Sunday between 1.00 pm and 4.00 pm, or by special arrangement. Telephone Tottington 3922 between 9.00 and 9.30 am or 10.00 and 10.30 pm.

Meanwhile, back to the summit of Crook Hill to continue our walk, we are seeking another famous packhorse track, the Limers Gate, whose interpretation into more general English means a road upon which lime was conveyed. This old moorland highway runs from Rochdale to Lancaster via Burnley, the northerly journey having been for coal carrying, whilst the return load was lime, for agricultural purposes. Here was the crude but efficient main road to North Lancashire before the Whitworth Valley was metalled; it was used by northbound Scotsmen deserting from the 1745 rebellion. The old packhorse track skirts the flank of Whitworth's Brown Wardle Hill, the most prominent hill in the area, almost pursuing the line of the old county boundary over Hades Hill and Freeholds Top, to drop into the beginnings of Sharneyford. Now it leaves the old boundary to penetrate deeper into Lancashire for its journey through Burnley.

Whitworth's Brown Wardle Hill is one of the best sites in the county for finds of Neolithic importance, its name indicating that this was once a look-out hill, used to observe the surrounding countryside for signs of raids by northern tribes, thus keeping safe the early Whitworth and Wardle Valley inhabitants.

Gentle pasture moors of fescue-grass, thistles and bog-rush supporting sheep, cattle and many horses are a feature of Hades Hill's westerly flank. Snipe and lapwing are also plentiful here during the nesting season, as are wheatears, which find the several tumbled drystone walls suitable for breeding sites. Over Hades Hill and Freeholds Top it is best to maintain a northerly route, by compass navigation. Soon, however, a recognisable Limers Gate is located making its way across the wilds of Reap's Moss,' a full cart-width and veering north west towards Sharneyford.

Lancashire's Reaps Moss adjoins Yorkshire's Inchfield Moor, which features an immaculate drystone wall of considerable length, eye-catching in its perfection. The Limers Gate is the old county boundary here, with splendid views down the valley sheep pastures towards Todmorden, where Yorkshire displays its muscle in the shape of Gorpley Reservoir and Stoodley Pike to the east. To the west is Lancashire's Rossendale Valley, once a royal hunting forest, where Pennine shepherds from far and wide assemble to take part in the Rossendale Lions Club sheepdog trials at Rawtenstall. It was here that I met Willie Heslop and 'Zak,' shepherd and sheepdog, who tend to the day-to-day running of Baxenden, a hill farm on the edge of the Rossendale Valley.

Willie's true occupation is as a sheepdog trainer rather than a shepherd, although obviously the one goes in hand with the other. "I breed sheep to train my dogs", Willie informed me, "rather than have dogs to work my sheep". Willie could only spare a moment to talk on this impor-

Above: The shepherd and his dog - a universally-appreciated image of country life. This is sheepdog trainer Willie Heslop and Zak, from the Rossendale Valley.

tant day. He was way ahead on points in the trials which is as good an advertisement for future business as one could hope to acquire. I stayed to watch Willie and 'Zak' complete an almost perfect run, and congratulated him on his return from the ring. "Zak's a good dog", he said, passing on the complement with a stroke to Zak's head. "I got three good sheep that were easy for Zak to handle, and I made the most of them. The temperament of the sheep are an important factor in sheepdog trials. Get a stubborn ewe which'll stand up to your dog and you're in trouble", he said.

Whilst Willie and I were chatting the next contestant, named Clarence, entered the ring to have an absolutely disastrous run. "I should have turned back this mornin' when yon magpie flew across front o' mi car", he said. "It's a sure sign o' bad luck for all t' day if a lone magpie crosses thi path, and I've proved it o'er an' o'er again". Turning to another shepherd who was listening to Clarence's comments, I said, "He's a suspicious gentleman, isn' he?" "Aye", he replied, "and he's a clever feller is Clarence. He's a feller worth listenin' to..."

And on that note of country folklore I departed to locate the Limers Gate at Sharneyford, where it is bisected by the A681 Bacup-Todmorden road. From here, the Limers Gate continues on the other side of the road for its journey to north Lancashire, taking in Heald Moor, Deerplay Moor, Burnley, Clitheroe and finally, Lancaster.

It was at Sharneyford that I spoke to a young man of modern times. Strolling along the A681, with his hands buried deep in his pockets was a youth with a punk haircut, cut in the style of a Mohican indian, and wearing all the iron-mongery associated with the style. On his approach I enquired: "Are there any inns in Sharneyford?"

"There's absolutely nowt in Sharneyford, mate," he replied, whilst simultaneously struggling with a strong wind, bent on destroying his dyed and lacquered locks. He was being careful to avoid being caught in a broadside blast. "If it's a pint you're after ,thi best bet is Sourhall, o'er Flowerscar, about two miles o'er yon moor". The OS map shows Flowerscar as Carr and Craggs and Todmorden Moor, across which a wild and windy packhorse track leaves the Limers Gate for the hamlet of Sourhall, again shown on the OS map as a nameless place with a cattle-grid and a public house.

I had heard about this isolated 16th century inn over the years, and had been fascinated by the tales of moormen who frequented its parlour. Rampant curiosity and a raging thirst demanded that I make this detour, and off I set across the beautiful virgin heather moorland of Flowerscar.

En route I recalled to mind some of the famed moorland characters of the past, such as the game-keeper whose favourite snack was a pound of tripe boiled in beer, accompanied by 18 slices of bread! Quite an appetite! It was an inn where plump pork sausages, frying in brown stout spat and sizzled throughout the day on the coal-fired stove, always at hand to satisfy the palates of cold, hungry moorland wayfarers, who spread the concoction on thick slices of bread with a communal knife. Herbert C. Collins in his book, *The Roof Of Lancashire*, lists four of these ravenous rovers as, John Tommy, Tom o' Mick's, Albert and Old John, names which suggest without further evidence being required that here was a quartet who would be unlikely candidates for tea at the vicarage. Practically all foods, including fish, was given the 'boiled in beer' or 'fried in stout 'treatment by these four connoisseurs of the *creme de la creme* in country cuisine, although Tom o' Mick's is reputed to have had an over-zealous appetite for the little-known delicacy of potato slices fried in goat fat. In fact in one of his more financially prosperous moments, it is said that he purchased a goat for ten shillings for this very purpose, and recalled with delight how he enjoyed, "tater slices cooked in nanny-goat fat fo' weeks after".

It wasn't many years after Herbert C. Collins met this outlandish foursome that the inn caught fire, and one suspects that the inn's then lethal culinary combination of a coal-fired stove continually being drenched in hot sausage fat could have had a great deal to do with the blaze!

Up hill and down dale, twisting and turning, the old packhorse track across Flowerscar had the makings of a fine big-dipper, with Sourhall down below sometimes in view and sometimes not. This track lends itself to deep thought, as indeed do most moorland jaunts, although in my case they were thoughts brought about by anticipation, of cool beer for a hot dry throat and a comfortable seat for aching limbs. Thoughts of the company I would soon be keeping, such as men dressed in well-worn tweeds, guns at their sides and Labrador dogs at heel, an open log fire and an atmosphere tainted with the smell of Brown Twist. Thoughts of seasoned moorland wayfarers, who could roll a cigarette with one hand whilst holding a pint of ale in the other and keep up a sensible conversation at the same time. A discussion centered around gun-dogs, the state of local grouse moors, poachers, troublesome vermin and all things rural would, thought I, be a welcome change from the more usual town or city public house talk.

'To Todmorden - To Portsmouth - Bacup Road', says a sign at the track's end, with 'The Old Dog and Partridge Inn', now renamed 'The Sourhall' (much less inspiring, I thought), standing opposite a line of cottages, painted brilliant white, looking very welcoming - and not open for another two hours!

"They don't open 'till about half seven in the evenings", a voice from an unknown source informed me. It originated from a hidden resident, bent low over his vegetable plot. Content to sit it out, I settled at the roadside, when the same voice inquired: "Had a long journey?"

"About eight miles today", I replied. "Well, eight miles is enough in this wind", he remarked. "We can't seem to get rid of this blasted wind this year". We talked for a while of bygone days in this remote district, and of the old stone-grinding wheel once sited in a field close by the inn. Turned on a pivot by a horse, it could grind stone fine enough for use on cottage floors before the days of household carpets. "They've gone and moved the grinding wheel to Bacup to put it on display", he said, whilst producing as if by magic a pint tumbler, full of cool orange-juice. "Will this help 'till Sourhall's open?" he asked with a knowing smile.

Orange-juice never tasted so good!

Eventually, I entered the Inn. No more a cosy parlour with an open log fire. No more the Twist-smoking moormen in tattered tweeds with a taste for sausages fried in stout. The old inn at Sourhall has literally been battered into the late 20th century, having had all of its interior rooms knocked into one large lounge. An extension provides a disco for Bacup and Todmorden youngsters. During my hour at the inn, unease was setting in as the ladies filed through the door for 'their' night.

"Male-stripper's not turned up yet!" bellowed the bow-tied Master of Ceremonies in a state of benign panic. The worst shock, however, came as I was perusing the *a la carte* menu, where I could neither find tripe boiled in beer nor sausages fried in stout. I finally settled for a packet of crisps and took the packhorse track at the side of the inn for the hamlet of Portsmouth, thinking as I walked of the days when pubs were pubs.

Passing the occasional house and a farmstead, the packhorse track is eventually lost to the walker when it joins a private road to yet another farmstead. At this point, a footpath across marshy ground breaks away from the packhorse track to skirt the farmstead; through lack of use this path has become overgrown and is also soon lost to the walker. Combined with mist, which is prevalent here, this terrain permits no alternative to map and compass navigation during which the intrepid walker must make the best of some very rough, swampy ground. This *Sphagnum* bog continues until meeting another farmstead, where a track through its farmyard leads to Cornholme and Portsmouth, in the Cliviger Gorge.

It was whilst crossing this *Sphag-*

Right: The village of Portsmouth, situated between Burnley and Todmorden in the Cliviger Gorge, on the old Lancashire county boundary, as seen from the neighbouring hill-tops.

num that I stumbled across a sickly sheep. Lying on its side and breathing heavily, no amount of my pushing and heaving would put it permanently back on 'all fours', occasionally a sound remedy. On explaining to a farmer of my discovery, he asked: "Was it an old sheep that you found?"

"Well", said I, "it wasn't a lamb, that's for sure". "Aye", said he, "sounds like an old 'un. You see the trouble is we can't afford to nurse sickly animals back to health, it's just not profitable". A harsh attitude in a harsh countryside!

Seen from the high, craggy flank of Cliviger Gorge, and painted gold by a summer sunrise, the hamlet of Portsmouth is a delightful sight to behold. It is situated between Burnley and Todmorden on the A646 (T) road, although our approach from the south is far less hectic that the motorist is accustomed to and can be described as positively peaceful.

Along a metalled lane, through slowly descending woodlands and streamlets, Portsmouth springs a surprise on the walker when it suddenly appears from behind a stand of trees.

There it is, tucked in the valley, its large village green and play area giving a pleasant first impression. Opposite to the green is a a post office and a fish and chip shop. At the green's easterly end is the excellent 'Glen View Inn', built in 1850 and maintaining that period's style throughout. Here at last is an inn that has not conformed to modern trends and where many a village tale is still told in its cosy parlour. "You mustn't stop for long in this village", remarked one patron of the inn. "Why not?" I enquired, thinking that I wasn't welcome. "Because they're dropping like bloody snow-flakes here at present", he said, referring to three sudden deaths in the village. Another talking point concerned a circular-saw operative who had just removed the top of his thumb in an unfortunate accident. "He tried to find the top of his thumb so that the surgeon could stitch it back on again at the hospital", said one concerned gentleman sitting at the bar, "but his dog had it before he could pick it up!" The silence was deafening as one and all tried to decide whether to remain straight-faced or explode in fits of laughter. The interlude of uncertainty was broken by a ruddy-faced Irishman holding a hand of dominoes: "It serves him right", he said, commanding everyone's attention and with little sympathy. "He was always bloody braggin' to me how that tripe-hound of his would eat owt he put in front of it!"

Named after the more widely-known seaport in Hampshire, Lancashire's Portsmouth finds that incoming mail which hasn't been post-coded invariably turns up at the South of England sorting office. Taking the names of places of repute appears to be a frequent habit in these parts - California is just a few miles down the road at Todmorden, where you will also find one of the most pleasantly situated cricket fields. Close to Portsmouth is the more industrialised hamlet of Cornholme, which has an excellent shop on the corner of Sun Terrace, next door to the 'Wagon and Horses' public house. Opening at 9.00 am, this shop offers take-away tea, hot chocolate, soup, and other drinks in sealed cups, together with a selection of pies and sandwiches. Having sampled the fare, I can fully recommend the shop. To leave Portsmouth for a northerly destination, locate 'The Roebuck' public house west of the hamlet, towards the tannery, whose chimney can be seen protruding from the hillside. Here, a lane sign-posted 'Kebs Road 1 1/4 miles' ventures over the tops to the Long Causeway, for which Kebs Road is a local name. This route takes the walker through oak-clad valleys and truly breathtaking scenery, although seldom trodden footpaths once again lose themselves in vegetation, or are indistinguishable

Below: The countryside between Portsmouth and the Long Causeway is chiefly cotton-sedge bog. Note the drystone walls, many in need of repair, which are very characteristic of the landscape hereabouts.

from the many sheep-tracks. Navigate by compass or follow the stream down the valley to Coat Clough Farm, which is marked on the OS map. From Coat Clough Farm a packhorse track runs to the Long Causeway across acre after acre of cotton-sedge which, in late June and early July, bursts into flower to transform a summer landscape into one more reminiscent of the first winter snows.

A glance at the OS map, and a little searching, will reveal the whereabouts of original Long Causeway pavement, sections thought of by modern-day standards as too hazardous for traffic, the contractors preferring to completely re-route the road across safer ground. One such stretch known as The Pavement crosses moor, marsh and the old county boundary close the Bank Top Farm; another stretch is found at Heptonstall. Packhorse men made good use of this ancient highway between Burnley and Halifax, repairing and restoring it where necessary, as did the Normans, the Vikings, the Danes, the Romans, and first and foremost Bronze Age man, who is also believed to have constructed the road in the first place. The route is still marked by the remnants of ancient crosses, which are believed to be of Celtic, Anglican or Norse origin, the best example being Mount Cross at the hamlet of Shore, the oldest religious monument hereabouts and said to be a replica of the Paulinus preaching crosses. Some authorities insist that Mount Cross displays Viking influences.

Upon reaching the Long Causeway, we follow the road's westerly direction, towards Burnley, for a few hundred yards to locate a small, fenced car-park, which boasts magnificent views across Worsthorne Moor and Black Hameldon. From here, a recently reinstated packhorse track sets off across the moor towards Far Pasture, which is a ruinous farmstead, to the hamlet of Hurstwood; to the east, the great arc of Black Hameldon supports the old county boundary. The hill does indeed appear to be black, or at least very dark in colour, when compared to its green and amber surroundings. Tucked in

Right: The old packhorse bridge near Hurstwood; a lasting monument to a traditonal builders craft.

the valley to our right is a small woodland, and in front, Cant Clough Reservoir. This is really wild scenery, accentuated by the fitting wild calls of curlews, and an area where Worsthorne Community Programme, aided by The Manpower Services Commission, is busily repairing walls, roads, bridges, and other moorland relics from the packhorse era.

The reinstated packhorse track expires at a renovated well situated amidst disused quarry workings. Cross the small brook close to the only drystone wall you see and walk in a north-westerly direction to pick up another packhorse track. Here a splendid packhorse bridge lures walkers like a magnet, on this particular occasion a party of Halifax naturalists. Accompanied by loud scoldings from a curlew, whose young it believed needed this protection, they explained their excitement at finding a short-eared owl's nest. "And this on our first visit to the area", remarked one of them.

Take the left track at the packhorse bridge for Far Pasture and Foxstones, the latter being a beautiful farmhouse set in a dip, and boasting an ancient well in its forecourt. This old well, which is a 'listed' structure and cannot be removed even though it impedes farm traffic, once had its own well-keeper, who lived in the adjacent barn. His duty was to draw water for the locals, and he is reputed to have said that he would never drink water from a lead pipe, maintaining that well-water was free of contamination and contributed to his good health. "Nobody told him", explained a farm worker, "that the well was fed by water flowing from the moor through a lead pipe. He died believing that he'd never tasted lead-contaminated water, when in truth he never drunk anything else!" At Foxstones, a sign at a gate reads:

'Private Road.' This is aimed at motorists, for this is the footpath to Hurstwood Village via Hurst Wood itself and the River Brun.

Legend tells of the Battle of Brunaburh, fought in 937 between the Danes and Saxons, after which the dead, including three kings, were buried here in the Brun Valley. A battle stone on the hill is said to mark the site of the skirmish. It was also the hills and cloughs of Hurstwood that persuaded Phillip Hamerton to set up his painters' camp and declare the Hameldon Hills to be "the best scenery to stir the senses". It was in this countryside that he completed many of his books.

Through the woods, over the bridged River Brun (which gave Burnley its name - originally "Brun Lea") and you stumble across Spenser's Cottage, set amidst colourful wild flowers, where Edmund Spenser, author of *The Faerie Queene,* just missed being born - his parents moved to London shortly before his birth! It is believed however, that return visits to Hurstwood and the Brun Valley eventually inspired him to put pen to paper. Just around the corner from Spenser's Cottage is Hurstwood Hall, built in 1579 by Barnard Towneley and his wife Agnes whose names appear over the door. *'Barnardus Towneley et agnes ejus 1579'* says the inscription. This small hamlet has changed little since that date, and the only outward signs of the 20th century are television aerials, telephone wires and, of course, camera-toting visitors.

Take the lane directly opposite to Hurstwood Hall's door, through the small, tastefully-built housing estate, whose gardens in summer drench the air with their fragrance, until meeting the sign-posted footpath for Worsthorne. This is a pleasant walk over flat pasture fields, which is unusual in this district of mountain and moor. The path terminates at Worsthorne's St John the Evangelist Church, by way of Green Terrace, which is situated in the village square alongside 'The Bay Horse' and 'The Crooked Billet' inns. You will also discover a general store, a fish and chip shop, a post office, a public telephone and toilets, and all conveniently located in the square.

Looking at sleepy Worsthorne today, it is difficult to picture the 17th century scene, when the hamlet was said to be infested with witches and boggarts. Obstinate children where thought of as 'Changelings' and small gifts of respect were left at known pixie playgrounds to console the little blighters. Bull-baiting and cock-fighting provided local sport, the last bull-

baiting being staged in 1834 next to the church, when Jim Anson's bull was defeated by Nick 'o' Ellis's dog, 'Crib.'

A conversation with a local grave-digger on my visit was an enlightening experience. On finding him digging in Worsthorne's churchyard, I asked if he would mind keeping an eye on my backpack whilst I stocked up with supplies at the general stores. "Certainly", he replied, sweating profusely. "I'll be on with this job for a while yet".

"They're not dropping like snowflakes here as well, are they?" I asked. "What do you mean?" said he. "I've just come from Portsmouth and I was told that three people had suddenly died there".

"They've not have they?" he said, looking somewhat concerned. "I've only just finished up that neck o' the

Below: A pleasant view of Worsthorne village, viewed through its church gates.

44

woods and it looks like I'll have to go back".

"Well, it's all money in your pocket", I replied. "Aye, but this is only supposed to be a part-time job," said the gravedigger. "I'm a miner, and I work for a private coal mining company during the week!"

He went on:"Follow Gorple Road for Briercliffe if you want a traffic-free walk." Running ruler-straight and heading directly east for the old county boundary on the summit of Black Hameldon, we take the last northerly path off Gorple Road, which is a left turn, close to a farmstead. This path passes a stone circle of Druid origin and a *tumulus,* the mystic moment of which is somewhat dampened by the presence of a refuse tip. Soon, however, Pendle Hill looms high in the western sky above Burnley to rekindle lost thoughts of witches and Druids. Swinden Reservoir is just half a mile away.

Situated above Swinden Reservoir on a steep and winding road, Briercliffe is a tiny hamlet of ribbon development, with a scattering of roadside cottages and a public house, the latter named the 'Roggerhamgate Inn.' In the dip of the road, a signs reads 'Ing Hey', which refers to a house, at the side of which is a metalled road leading via a farmstead to Extwistle Moor. Once through the farmstead, take a right turn to travel hard by the reservoir, ignoring the quarry road, and notice the outline of Twist Castle Roman Camp on the northerly flank - a huge mound and a different shade of green mark its whereabouts. This area is a hive of the doings of primitive hill-men, with *tumuli,* stone circles and earthworks round nearly every turn. Walking hard by the reservoir results in a dead end at a drystone wall; pursue the drystone wall uphill for 100 yards to relo-

cate the footpath and a stile.

Our three most noticeable companions on this section of the walk are scolding curlews, the ever-present bulk of Pendle Hill and a wind strong enough to buffet the body. Eventually, the footpath forks into two rough tracks, one to the left (our route) continuing through quarry workings, passing *tumuli* and ancient earthworks towards popular Thursden Brook. Thursden looks best from the rocky outcrop above Widdop Reservoir road, which is a metalled packhorse track, open to motorists and linking the towns of the Colne Valley with Hebden Bridge. There are no facilities at Thursden Brook, although this doesn't prevent summer weekends seeing it well populated by those who wish to relax for a few hours in sylvan surroundings. "That's what we like about Lancashire", remarked an American couple enquiring as to the whereabouts of Downham and Waddington. "Your towns suddenly end and your countryside suddenly begins - and make sure you keep it that way!" We must hope that our county planners think the same way.

The Widdop Reservoir road adjoins two secondary roads servicing the Colne Valley. Marked on the OS map as 'Cattle Grids', our road forks to the right and is a steep climb (flanked by conifer plantations) which terminates upon reaching the footpath across the moor to Trawden and Wycollar. A five-barred gate to the right of the road junction marks the path's location. Initially, we are walking on comfortable pasture moor, but this slowly but surely changes to rough, tussocky moorland which grips the boots as we climb to Will Moor. Here, the path enters the doorway of a remnant farmstead's gable-end, the only part left standing; its huge doorway lintel of shaped stone is all

Right: The unspoiled beauty of Thursden Brook, between Hebden Bridge and the Colne Valley. This is marvellous place in which to 'get away from it all' and escape for an hour or two from the hustle and bustle of the 20th century.

Facing page: The rather sad spectacle of the lone farmhouse gable end, to be found on Will Moor. What stories could this ancient doorway tell?

of four feet across. At dusk, when cast in silhouette, this gable-end on the lonely moor echoes of the macabre, where a 'Dance of Death' or a strange medieval religious rite would not seem out of place.

Once through the doorway of the eerie gable-end, the footpath of Trawden, Wycollar and Haworth is marked by posts bearing yellow arrows, which terminate at a pack-horse track. Follow the track to the right to meet the newly-stoned path leading to the Bronte Way of Wycollar, a path whose snake-like course across wild, beautiful countryside can seemingly be traced to infinity. This can be an off-putting sight to the already leg-weary walker, who realises that a simple four inches on the OS map can in reality (and when seen to its end) be a soul-destroying four miles!

During this walk to Wycollar, you will come across a steep dip in the track, with a stream in the bottom, which has been piped to prevent flooding during periods of heavy rain. From this plastic pipe flows the

coolest and sweetest of moorland waters, and it is a welcome discovery indeed on a hot summer's day, on what appears to be a road with no end. Enjoy the clear water by all means - but please add a *Puritab* or other water-purification tablet to your canteen, just to be on the safe side. This isn't the ideal place to suffer an upset stomach!

This countryside is of rolling bog pastures, with creeping buttercups, thistles and various bog rushes racing down in the north-west into the bottoms of the Colne Valley, whilst to the south-east the journey is upwards to 1,700ft and the much more hard-bitten moors of Lad Law and Jackson's Ridge, both on the old county boundary. Collectively, this impressive arc of moorland is known as Boulsworth Hill and it is a wilderness which is unfortunately devoid of footpaths. It was the home of Neolithic man - and some people insist that it still is, if reports of strange sightings are anything to go by. A report of one sighting in 1985 reads: "I had started my descent in the dusk, when I glanced back at a

huddle of standing and leaning stones. There, lurching forward and then quickly drawing back into the shadows, I saw an apeman figure". This glance at a ghost of pre-history no doubt warranted a much hastier descent than was originally intended!

Eventually, the path's stone surface is replaced by original packhorse pavement, which is easy on the feet and silently speaks volumes for the road-building abilities of the hardy packhorse drovers. Who better than these early moorland wayfarers to teach local authorities about moorland track construction? It certainly proves that covering original packhorse track pavement with crippling gravel-chips is a mistake. Here is splendid walking into what can only be described as some of the most impressive countryside in the county. We are at the beginnings of Wycollar Beck, where all footpaths are clearly marked to lead the walker down the beautiful wooded valley to where the Beck meets the lane to accompany it through the village.

Wycollar Beck is born high in Boulsworth's wild and forgotten wastes, being slowly nurtured to maturity by several rushing streamlets, glasslike in clarity and passing sites of natural architecture such as Steeple Stones and Grey Stones, two names which reflect this tough, uncompromising terrain. Crow Hill lies on the old county boundary, and does indeed harbour the carrion crow, the whole of this area being a westerly-facing, brackened flank, which emits a glorious golden hue when seen in the soft light of a Pendle sunset. It is important to contain visits to this time of day to fully appreciate this magnificent countryside, when you will also be enchanted by the dusk summer songs of woodland birds, including blackbirds, song thrushes, chaffinches and willow warblers, which voice their opinions from the oak-clad, lower reaches of Wycollar Beck. It is a feast of natural sight and sound.

The wet, sedgy pastures of the Beck's southerly slopes are under natural rather than agricultural control. Throughout the summer months here is a confusion of colourful flowering plants, and in sufficient variety to bewilder younger 'townies', who will probably have never seen the like, and which will remind older visitors of the England of their childhood. Boulder-piled walls preceded the drystone wallers' skills and tell of the activity of primitive hill-men, who eagerly claimed land and just as eagerly enclosed it, using the materials at hand. In this case, huge boulders of four and five feet across and placed as base stones to support boulders of a lesser size. One is left wondering at the strength of these wild moormen, especially when we are taught that their diet left a great deal to be desired, and that their knowledge of construction was severely limited. The enthusiasm, however, with which they tackled what must have appeared to be the most daunting of tasks is a lesson for us all.

Knee-deep in cotton-sedge, buttercups and campion, the valley taking Wycollar Beck winds its way down to the village, the beck itself widening at every ripple to accommodate the amounts of accumulated water, yet remaining shallow enough for dippers and grey wagtails to explore insect *larvae*. All will eventually empty into Colne Water at Laneshaw Bridge to begin a journey through the industrial valley beyond.

Another name for Boulsworth's north-westerly foothills is 'The Forest of Trawden', a one-time hunting forest governed by Edward the Confessor rather than a forest of trees, as we today understand the word.

Although the valleys provide the exception to the rule, woodlands have always been few and far between in this landscape of standing stones and muddy morass, the most common habitat being of sturdy sedges, grasses and brackens, which possess the constitution needed to weather the harshest of winters on the poorest of soils. The rowan or mountain ash is the only tree to be seen on the bracken slopes, and these can be counted on the fingers of one hand; they lack any hint of healthy growth, with drab and drooping foliage complementing bared, withered roots. Tree life here is moribund and soon will be no more.

Harsh also describes a law introduced here by James I, who forbade the use of manures on the land, declaring that the tenant farmers were merely tolerated in the royal hunting forest and not worthy of their occupation if they had to resort to soil fertilisation for successful crops. The land was known as *assart,* which permitted the farmers only to grub up whins and shrubs to clear the ground and very little else; crop failures resulted in the land being returned to the crown. James required the forest solely for hunting, and he didn't take into account at first the loss of revenue to the crown that his reckless actions would bring about. On feeling his empty purse, however, he soon relented, and granted tenants a 12-year lease and permission to use manures in random amounts if necessary.

A keen ornithological ear at this location may pick out the summer trills of nesting dunlin on the slopes of Pot Brinks Moor and Broad Head Moor, two of the very few places in the county where this species breeds - and secure for some time to come if rough, private terrain is any protection. The twite, or mountain linnet,

prefers less severe moorland than its name implies, keeping to the lower, more wind-free pasture moors here. This has much to do with the twite's favourite food, the seeds of wild plants, particularly those of knapweed and thistle, which are absent (or less plentiful) on the gale-swept stony summits which have only a veneer of top-soil. The Scots know the twite as the yellow-neb lintie which, when translated, means yellow-billed linnet, and gives a clue to the bird's most distinctive feature.

A Burnley ornithologist explained to me that merlin and hen harrier are regularly seen hunting the Boulsworth slopes during the summer months, which is evidence enough to suggest that breeding is in progress. Both species favour ling and mixed bracken moors, the wilder the better, and with little disturbance, making Boulsworth a suitable habitat on all counts. "What about winter?" I asked. "Are there any sightings worth mentioning?"

"Not so many people venture up here during winter", he replied, "although parties of snow buntings have been seen now and again. It can be rather wicked up here in winter time".

Boulsworth Hill, just like other winter black spots in the Pennines, has taken several lives in years past, and during the 18th and 19th centuries, the winter Pennines were claiming so many lives that it initiated a new attraction at remote moorland inns, whose innkeepers would display the dead on the bar for their customers' pleasure. The 'Moorcock Inn' on Rochdale's Rooley Moor, was particularly noted for this type of exhibition, and so good for custom was this 'laying out' that a reward was offered to those who brought a body to the inn for display. This created a type of bounty-hunting in the

Right: A grouse shoot-ing party at Boulsworth Hill, near Burnley.

Pennine uplands, when known notorious areas were painstakingly searched following spells of heavy snow, with Boulsworth's lost and lonely byways being top of the list. On discovering a body, it was thrown unceremoniously across the back of a packhorse and taken to a chosen inn, whence the innkeeper would send messages to surrounding valley towns and hamlets to tell of his latest bar attraction, with 'great quantities of beer being brewed for the expected rush of customers'.

Boulsworth's countryside deserves far more attention than time will permit. It is vast and impressive, dwarfing all around it, including the industrial towns of the Colne Valley, which are no more than dots on the landscape by comparison when seen from this lofty vantage point. Visit it, and enjoy the marvellous landscape.

Wycollar's claim to fame, apart from its immediately apparent beauty, is its three ancient bridges. The oldest one, and the first one we encounter when walking down the village lane, is a single-monolith stone bridge of prehistoric origin and weighing many tons. Over the years, this bridge has tested the strength of many a sturdy moorman, each one convinced that he possessed the muscle and bone required to dislodge it from its seemingly precarious position. None have succeeded to date. The next bridge is constructed of three huge stone slabs, supported by two boulders, and dating from the pre-Roman era. Finally, close to the cobbled ford that crosses the Beck, is a magnificent 13th century double-arched pack-horse bridge, so narrow, so twisted and so completely out of true as to be thoroughly appealing to all who see it.

Also close to the ford is Wycollar Hall, now a roofless ruin. Built by the Hartley family in the 16th century, it was extended in the 18th century by Henry Owen Cunliffe, who resided here until his death in 1818. Following his death, the hall was practically taken apart by local inhabitants needing building stone for their own premises - one house boasts the hall's original porch and pillars. Wycollar Hall still contains its huge

Facing page: The tranquil and relaxing beauty of Wycollar. This is the village's triple slab bridge, dating from the pre Roman era.

Facing page: Wycollar's 13th century packhorse bridge, over which a spectral horseman has been seen to ride, according to village legend. In the background are the ruins of Wycollar Hall. This village is one of Lancashire's finest, and a personal favourite of mine.

Left: Wycollar is very much a village of interesting bridges, and this single monolith is a structure of ancient origin. Many a sturdy moorman has atempted to dislodge the bridge from its seemingly precarlous boulder position. None have succeeded to date.

fireplace, although this is now believed to have been a late introduction, and more for ornamental than practical use. The hall is believed to have been the inspiration behind Charlotte Bronte's Ferndean Manor in her novel 'Jane Eyre'. Charlotte Bronte wandered this way on many occasions from her home across the moor at Haworth, a route now recognised as the 'Bronte Way'.

At Christmastime, a spectre horseman is said to visit the hall, the clatter of spectral hoofs on the old packhorse bridge accompanied by a woman's scream proclaiming that he has arrived. He is reputedly a member of the Cunliffe family returning to the scene of a murder he committed at the hall. The village is also said to be haunted by a cat which chooses to tread thin air by walking two feet off the floor!

Perspiring, parched and feeling somewhat ponderous following several hours of rough walking, I arrived in Wycollar at 8.30 pm on a summer Sunday evening. My backpack contained little else other than accumulated rubbish where food and water should be, and I anticipated a supperless night, with plans to buy supplies in Trawden the next day - Sunday closing makes the seventh day a sorrowful day in the backpackers' calendar! A party of family and friends were having their photographs taken whilst paddling in Wycollar

Beck, close to the ford, when a gentleman, on noticing my camera-bag asked: "Excuse me, but what light-reading do you get here?" Convinced that his camera was faulty, I explained that the onset of dusk was responsible for his low light-reading, and asked the whereabouts of the nearest inn. "The Herders Arms is about one and half miles away," he replied. "Or you can choose from two inns in Trawden, which is the same distance". He thought for a while and suggested that I try the village Craft Shop, which also has a small cafe. "If good food and a pot of hot tea will do instead of a pint, you'll not find any better", he remarked.

It sounded marvellous, and it was. A pot of piping-hot tea, together with a Cornish pasty, red cabbage, peas and a saucer of raw onion to add to taste cost a very reasonable £1.00! Opening at 10.30am seven days a week, and only closing when all visitors have departed, here also is a very handy place of refreshment for walkers.

Although Wycollar is now classed as a country park, it is in reality a working agricultural community, whose picturesque village is simply being restored following decades of neglect. It is a village of old hand-loom weavers' cottages dating from the 17th century, having changed little since that time and very popular with tourists from all points of the globe, particularly Australia and the United States of America. What you won't find in Wycollar is a litter-bin. "Because we don't have any litter", a cottager informed me when I asked for the whereabouts of a 'bin' for my rubbish. Nor will you find chips or beefburgers on sale at the Craft Shop cafe. "Because we don't want the smell," I was told. "Visitors don't expect a 'Blackpool' atmosphere when they come to Wycollar", the Craft Shop proprietor informed me, "but rather the very best in Lancashire village life". Looking at the comments in Wycollar's Visitors' Book, all of which (with the solitary exception of one amusing Australian!) extol the virtues of the village, it appears that visitors appreciate the hamlet just the way it is. The Australian? He extolled the virtues of the cafe's waitress! Well, like I said, he was Australian....

Wycollar owes much of its present-day appeal to the 'Friends of Wycollar', an action-group formed in the 1950s to arrest the decay of their village, which was described at the time as being "almost derelict." They couldn't have imagined in their wildest dreams that their dynamic endeavours would finally result in Wycollar being given country park status. Quite a success story.

My mid-evening arrival at Wycollar Village didn't permit time for bed and breakfast accommodation to be sought. On explaining to the Craft Shop proprietor of my pilgrimage along Lancashire's old county boundary, and my immediate predicament, arrangements were made for me to camp in the country park for the night. His generosity was again demonstrated when he walked to my campsite, to deliver a few matches. I had pitched my tent on a high wooded knoll overlooking the huge, black mass of Pendle Hill, and a good half-a-mile of uphill walking from his village home; it was a kindly gesture, which I much appreciated. The Craft Shop doesn't sell matches, and this permitted a pipe of tobacco to be enjoyed whilst watching the 'Big End' of Pendle greedily devouring a crimson, setting sun. He told me how he and his wife had just sold their Burnley home and abandoned secure jobs to take on the new business venture of owning Wycollar's Craft

Shop, a somewhat risky move and one which depends upon the hamlet attracting tourists all the year round to be successful. We wish them well in their new lives in one of the county's most captivating villages.

Monday morning, 5.00 am, brought nothing to suggest that, just eight hours earlier, a burning red sun had produced beads of perspiration on my brow as it sank behind the western hills. The old nautical saying came to mind: 'Red sky at night, sailors' delight', which now smacked of the amateur weather-forecaster like never before,for I peered from my tent to witness Pendle Hill wearing a veil of black and menacing rain-clouds, as if in mourning for me and the countryside around it. Cloud-wrack was blowing down the hill-sides towards Wycollar, much like tumbleweed rolls off a windy desert, heavy with moisture and appearing more solid than vaporous in structure. My tent covering heaved and flapped in the gale and intermediate bouts of torrential rain which, thankfully, ceased just as quickly as they began. This vile weather lasted for more than four hours, subjecting my new *Trekker* tent to a thorough testing; thankfully, it came through with 'flying colours.' The *Trekker* is a one-man tent weighing just 3lbs, and measuring just 13in x 7in when packed. Available from your local *Famous Army Stores,* at around £50.00 it is a sound purchase and can be fully recommended for the solitary walker and camper who likes to sleep beneath the stars.

By 10.00 am all climactic chaos had calmed, the now-still air being inject-ed with warm sunlight which cast long shafts of shimmering iridescence through Wycollar Hall's glass-less, mullioned windows. Pendle Hill, now glistening in pea-green, looked its old self once again, echoing the words of Jessica Lofthouse when she wrote: "No hill uses its inches better than Pendle Hill". Over the years many literary luminaries have enthused about Pendle Hill, or 'Burnley's Mountain,' as it is some-times known, describing its magnifi-cence from all points of the county. And why not? It is seven miles long, 1,832 feet high, and utterly majestic; it will be our constant companion until we lose sight of it in the boggy bowels of Bowland Forest, many miles further on along the old county boundary.

A breakfast of two boiled eggs, toast and coffee preceded my goodbyes and extending my warm thanks to Wycollar's Craft Shop proprietor and his wife. I left their cafe to be imme-diately greeted with a, "Good morning to you, sir" from a gentleman in wild-west attire and sporting a Texan drawl. Not quite what you expect in Wycollar. "Would you mind if I took your photograph?" he asked, whilst fumbling with the controls of his Nikon camera.

"Not at all", I replied, "although I am only a visitor here like yourself". This didn't dissuade him from his intent on capturing me for posterity, placing me firmly against a cottage wall and per-mitting his camera's motor-drive to run riot, running off film at five frames per second. "Thank you, sir. Have yourself a good day", he wished me in true American style, and set off with his eyes focussed on a lady cot-tager who was shaking a rug at her gate, who I have no doubt turned out to be his next 'victim.'

The old county boundary is just one and a half miles north-east of Wycollar, having made an acute turn to the north-west when it 'bounced off 'the cairn of Combe Hill, close to Wolf Stones. We will rejoin it approxi-mately two miles further on.

Chapter 3

CROSS COUNTRY TO PENDLE

LEAVING behind the charms of Wycollar will undoubtedly bring a tear to the eye of those with an affinity for beautiful, unspoiled country villages. Not everyone thinks the same way of course, and a builder acquaintance of mine explained how he purchased and completely renovated a Wycollar cottage, only to experience great difficulty in selling it. He finally had to settle for a substantial financial loss in order to dispose of it: the quiet isolation of a 17th century village, it appears, is for many people, more for permanent admiration than permanent accommodation.

Our route to Laneshaw Bridge from Wycollar follows the Trawden road for a short distance to pick up an open country footpath, the whole journey being just a matter of tracing the course of Wycollar Beck. Passing between an eye-catching white cottage and the Beck, the path crosses the Beck at an old stone bridge, from where a left turn locates a stile-to-stile walk to Laneshaw Bridge. The meandering Wycollar Beck is never far away from the footpath, although it does occasionally wriggle into an S-bend from time to time.

Unlike previous parts of our route, there isn't anything gaunt or gritty about this landscape. No jagged outcrops jut menacingly from grey, gritstone summits to interrupt this skyline, and there are no sinister standing stones to add a dash of the macabre to the dusk horizon. The high hills are still there, yet they are of a more friendly persuasion, having a sleek, emerald green appearance, lush in pasture grasses and dotted here and there with black and white cattle. The lower pastures at this point are prone to regular soakings by Wycollar Beck, which from time to time, spills its excesses into what have now become swampy dells. Come here in early September to see a golden show of monkey flower, a show so strikingly vivid that its brilliance beneath a noon-day sun almost stings the eyes.

To the front, the grey stone cottages of Laneshaw Bridge hang on the hillside, whilst to the west, as we have now become accustomed, towers the rounded whale's-back of 'Old Man Pendle,' deep purple in colour and adrift in character from all other hills around it. Wycollar Beck will shortly lose its independence when it flows into Colne Water and the River Laneshaw, to mark the meeting place of three rivers.

Laneshaw Bridge is an ancient place with an equally ancient Holy Well. In AD 926 King Athelstan, whilst on his travels across his kingdom, boasted that he " ruled all the kings in the land and at a place called Eamot they renounced idolatry". The place name 'Eamot' refers to today's Emmott, (which is marked on the OS map) to show the former location of Emmott Hall, built in 1737 and now demolished, and also the site of the Holy Well. The well is a substantial structure of stone and its waters, which reputedly possess healing powers, still attracts pilgrims. In AD 835, many early Christians were baptised here.

Another noteworthy Laneshaw Bridge resident of past years was the stunning Bonny Hannah Corbrick, a buxom beauty who brought a twinkle to many a local farm-lad's eye. Nevertheless, as is so often the case, she gave her heart to a mindless ne'er-do-well, a man of debased

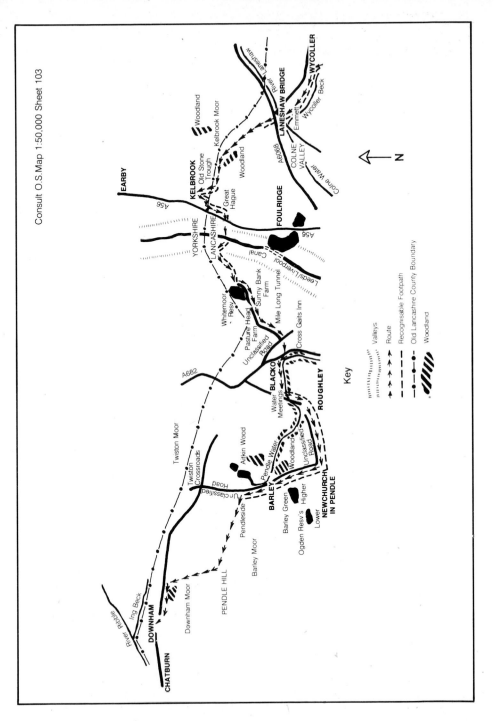

Consult O.S. Map 1:50,000 Sheet 103

CHATBURN
DOWNHAM
River Ribble
Ing Beck
Downham Moor
PENDLE HILL
Twiston Moor
Twiston Crossroads
Unclassified Road
Pendleside
Barley Moor
Atkin Wood
Pendle Water
BARLEY
Barley Green
Ogden Resv's
Higher
Lower
NEWCHURCH IN PENDLE
Woodland
Unclassified Road
ROUGHLEY
BLACKO
Water Meetings
A682
Unclassified Road
Pasture Head Farm
Whitemoor Resv.
Sunny Bank Farm
Cross Gaits Inn
Mile Long Tunnel
Leeds/Liverpool Canal
YORKSHIRE
LANCASHIRE
EARBY
A56
KELBROOK
Old Stone Trough
Great Hague
Woodland
Kelbrook Moor
Woodland
FOULRIDGE
A56
A6068
LANESHAW BRIDGE
River Laneshaw
WYCOLLER
Wycoller Beck
Emmett
COLNE VALLEY
Colne Water

Key

Valleys
Route
Recognisable Footpath
Old Lancashire County Boundary
Woodland

N

57

morals who would beat her in public and commit her to ridicule for his own pleasure. This she endured until, finally, in one of his more drunken rages, he went too far with a beating and killed her. He then carried her body onto the moor and lay her in a shallow grave close to Barnside. Bonny Hannah Corbrick's tormented ghost is said to have haunted the moors hereabouts for years after the incident, and to such an extent that it pricked the conscience of one particular villager, who organised a search to seek out her remains. Eventually her body was discovered and exhumed for re-burial. She now rests peacefully in Colne churchyard and her spirit hasn't been seen since.

On a more down-to-earth note, it was whilst I was standing at the meeting place of Colne Water, the River Laneshaw and Wycollar Beck, that I encountered five schoolboy ramblers and, as is the way of 12 and 13 year -olds, all were prone to harmless mischief. " What tha doin' in yon watter, mister?" asked one seemingly cocky youngster. Removing my camera from eye-level I explained that I was photographing the cottages along Carriers Row. "Well", he said, as he rubbed his chubby friend's curly hair, "tak a picture o' this fat bugger when tha's done that - that's if tha can fit 'im in!" With this remark all signs of friendship abruptly disappeared and sides were immediately chosen, with all five of them disappearing over the river embankment in a frenzy of rucksack-bashing and name-calling. Once over the final stile meeting the lane at Laneshaw Bridge, turn right along the lane (Carriers Row) to accompany the River Laneshaw for a short distance to School Lane. Turn left along School Lane to see the Emmott Arms on the rise. This is the A6068 Colne-

Keighley road and the centre of Laneshaw Bridge Village, which provides shops for those in need of supplies. A right turn along the A6068 soon locates a public footpath sign reading: "Public Footpath to Black Lane Ends - 2 Miles". The path squeezes between a River Laneshaw tributary and a cottage gable-end, passing beneath overhanging trees, which almost conceal the route. It is a follow-your-nose, stile-by-stile course, passing through an old mill yard and through Shaw Gate Farm, marked on the OS map. Once through this Farm, take the roughly-stoned track bending to the left to meet a country lane with a cattle-grid and a line of white cottages. Turn right here and walk for 50 yards to locate a footpath sign, again on your right. Our route is the concrete road towards Flass Bent, marked on the OS map, which is a left turn immediately before and almost opposite to the footpath sign.

The residents of this beautiful rolling countryside maintain the renowned Lancashire tradition for friendship and politeness to strangers, especially, it appears, to lost and lonely wayfarers such as me! "I'm going as far as Skipton if that'll help", said one motorist as he drew alongside in his Rangerover. Shortly after: "Can I give you a lift to the top of the lane?" asked a farm-worker at Shaw Gate Farm. I explained to both kind offers that I was walking the old Lancashire county boundary. "Rather you than me, mate", said my new-found Rangerover friend, "but I hope you have a good time". The farm-worker at Shaw Gate Farm scrutinised my route on the map, directed me along the Flass Bent path, and then sped away with the words:" Have a pint for me in every village along the way". Nice people. Pursuing the concrete road through the small farmyard at

Flass Bent eventually locates an opening in a drystone wall at the yard's far end. This opening leads to a stone stile, set in another drystone wall, which can be clearly seen across the rough pasture. Once over the stile, turn right to climb the rushy moor to the ridge of Great Edge.

This is a green, gleaming landscape, where contrasting black drystone walls separate the pastures to produce uniform squares, giving the whole area a giant chequer-board appearance. The only draughts to be encountered here, however, are the type that race through the rushes to chill the cheeks or nip through the nicks of a neglected stone wall. Curlews, carrion crows and countless sheep make most of the moves here, the latter also making most of the noise with their continual bleating. "Wear British Wool - 35 Million Sheep can't be Wrong!" informed a slogan in the window of a tractor's cab.

The intensity of sheep grazing here, combined with shifting peat deposits and rampant growths of bog-moss, have long since obliterated any visible signs of what were obviously seldom-trodden footpaths. The stiles, however, are still present to prove that footpaths once existed. It is best to navigate by compass, choosing a roughly west-of-north route from the summit of Great Edge, from where the route will terminate at a drystone wall and fenced-off, flooded delph. Follow the drystone wall to your left to locate a stile and a visible path leading across pastures towards a woodland and Kelbrook Moor, both on the old county boundary.

With the old county boundary once again in view, I leapt over this stile with a spring in my step. I quickly returned, however, with the speed of a seasoned sprinter and pursued by Boris, who was frothing-at-the mouth. Boris, if you haven't guessed already,

is a highly sensitive Herefordshire bull, a huge rusty-brown creature with the physique of a Churchill tank. On noticing my approach, he thundered over the ground in riotous hot pursuit, seeing this intruder back over the wall without a word of protest, after which he proudly returned at a trot to his harem.

Boris's somewhat forceful suggestion to seek an alternative path to Kelbrook Moor resulted in my having to trespass - he occupied and vehemently guarded the only public footpath in our direction. Much better, thought I, to suffer the indignity of castigation than the seething side-effects of concussion, and so over the wall and across the private pasture I stealthily trod. Whilst looking furtively around me, I noticed a black and white sheep-dog running in my direction, followed by a lithe farmer carrying a stout stick. The way my luck was running, it was almost a certainty that the dog would take the seat out of my pants prior to a clout from the farmer's stick!

As the dog was at the point of running down its quarry, namely me, the farmer let out an ear-piercing whistle and a yell: "Shep!" he bellowed, with such high-pitched intensity that the sound echoed around the valley. The dog stopped dead in its tracks, lay down and fixed me with its gaze until his master arrived at his side. "You've some fine pasture land here", said I in an attempt to mellow the moment. He looked me straight in the eyes and nodded his head: "It's a bit o'alright is this, isn't it?" he replied, which took me totally by surprise. Once again I explained about my county boundary journey, and how Boris had offered little choice but to trespass. "Oh, the big Hereford", he said between laughs. "If yon big fella got his horns into thi, that wouldn't need bother about paths - he'd launch thi onto Kelbrook Moor!"

We chatted about various country matters, from sheep parasites, known as flukes, to the advantages and disadvantages of farming such a beautiful area. The disadvantages? "We're blocked in come the first snow-fall, and life's a matter o' livin from day to day after that," said the farmer. He explained how the late 20th century had yet to 'catch up' with their farming policy: "We're only little fellers here". he mused. "We're little fellers livin' on little wages 'cos we only have little fields, but we wouldn't ha' it any other way". He pondered for a while and then suggested that, "There's a lot more to life than just money, although it musn't be bad bein' a millionaire!"

We returned to the subject of the belligerent Herefordshire bull, which included his own remedy for consoling the beast; "Bulls like bein' cock o' the roost", he explained," "and thee venturin' o'er 'is land posed a threat to this. It's just same wi' farmers tha knows. Bulls don't knowt' difference between farmers and your hikers, and they'll ha' a go at farmers as weel as you". By this time I had found a true friend in his dog, Shep, which had settled on my left foot to gain easier access to my stroking hand. "Tha can't calm a bull down wi' doin' that, tha knows", he remarked, pointing down to Shep with his stick. "Tha mun grab owd o' yon ring in its nose for't' calm 'im down, and then tha can lead 'im about like a lamb". This course of action to get the better of a bull prompted an obvious question: "What would happen if I went for the ring in its nose, and missed?" I asked. "Oh tha's not for't' miss", he replied. "Tha can do owt but miss, owd lad", he went on. "If that just happen for't' miss and tha can't run a lick tha'd be in trouble, that's for sure, and I don't

think that could run so quick wi' yon big bag on thi back!"

Soon it was map-scrutinising time again, with my route being amended for the umpteenth time. "Tha mun tak' a look at yon old shooting-lodge", he advised. "It's just yon by that road, and tha can get to it through yon gate o' mine along th' edge o' mi pasture". So ended a pleasant and instructive half-hour with a humorous and very understanding farmer. He left me with a hand-shake and good wishes for the remainder of my journey, and also with the local knowledge that, "There's nowt on Kelbrook Moor for't' interest thi readers, only heather, and tha can see that any time tha's a mind to. Tha'll be much better of telling' 'em about yon shooting-lodge than maulin' up Kelbrook Moor".

Reminiscent in architectural design to one of the better Scottish shooting-lodges, and situated just off the lane that skirts the woodland below Kelbrook Moor, this particular shooting-lodge plays host to clay-pigeon shooters rather than grouse-shooters. Someone, I was informed, had just purchased the lodge, although for what purpose wasn't generally known. It is such an unusual, even quaint building, tall and compact with steps leading up to the porched doorway, that it wouldn't surprise me to see this shooting-lodge turned into a permanent place of residence.

Had the Herefordshire bull not impeded my path, the original route would have skirted the easterly flank of the woodland below Kelbrook Moor, from where one has a choice of climbing to Kelbrook Moor's cairn or taking the lane via the shooting-lodge. On this occasion, I was left with no alternative but to trespass, which meant taking the shooting-lodge route, although it must be borne in mind that setbacks in the nature of bulls are only temporary inconveniences at certain times of the year. The chances of meeting a jealous bull like Boris in mid summer are pretty remote. In consequence, I will explain the course of the original route to the shooting-lodge which, as mentioned earlier, is the only public footpath heading in our direction.

Once over the stile which we can call Boris's Stile, keep hard by the drystone wall, following its line until locating the joining of four paths close to the farmhouse. Take the left path towards Oxenards, which is marked on the OS Map. This path penetrates a beautiful section of the woodland to run into a roughly-stoned track, where, after a quarter of a mile or so, you will see on your right the shooting-lodge. Here, almost adjoining the shooting-lodge drive, a farm-track branches to your right, heading in a north-westerly direction. Continue through the farmyard for a stile-to-stile walk to the country lane servicing the hamlet of Kelbrook. A compass reading should be north from the first stile for approximately two hundred yards, which will bring you to a five-barred gate with a simple rope fastening arrangement. From here the direction is north-west to the lane.

It is interesting to note how the Lancashire dialect becomes more and more evident as we enter the districts of Nelson and Colne, Burnley and Pendle, and how it is at its peak in the remote, country areas where the 20th century and its trappings have been less influential. Many country folk in these Pennines still refer to Burnley as Brunley which, in every respect, is the correct pronunciation and just a continuation of the name, Brun, the town's founder river. A map drawn in the year 1610, "The Countie Pallatine of Lancaster", displays Burnley as Brunley, which

makes one wonder why only the town has become subject to mis-pronunciation. The River Brun and the Brun Valley have maintained their originality in both print and the spoken word, while 'Brunley' hangs only by the fraying thread of an older generation and soon, doubtless, it will be heard no more.

As I passed by, one of this older generation of moorland farmers was at the task of repairing a drystone wall close to Thick Bank. I was admiring the huge arc of Kelbrook Moor which, in early September, is crowned with a purple hood of flowering heather and forms the easterly horizon in these parts, when I noticed him juggling with various stones and studying each one with a searching eye. On noticing my approach, he straightened his back and mopped his brow, cast down a stone and bid me a good afternoon. I returned the friendly gesture and remarked at the fine display of heather on Kelbrook Moor. "Aye", he said, whilst arching his back, "but it's not like yon every year. Some years it's as dark and miserable as yon owd mon o'er theer". He was pointing at Pendle Hill which, to my eye, looked resplendent beneath a sky of duck-egg blue. "I don't know what's happened to it this year for't gi' a show like yon", he continued, "but tha can bet that's it for a few years". A healthy heather moor in these parts should, of course, support a healthy grouse population. There's nowt like that on theer", he said. "Yon clay-pigeon shooters scare 'em off wi' their racket. They're at it every week-end and, as tha probably knows, grouse won't put up wi' that kinda goings on". With this he proceeded with the rebuilding of the wall, and then thought better of it. "I'll stick a pallet in yon hole for' time bein'", he murmured, and then quietly sauntered up the pasture with long, leggy strides towards the farmhouse.

I sat beside the ruinous drystone wall, unwrapped my sandwiches, and watched as I ate how the old farmer and his sombre work-a-day attire slowly merged with the hues of the countryside - he was lost from sight long before reaching his cottage. How different, I thought, are the folk that live and work on the moors to those hikers who visit from towns at weekends, and embellish themselves beforehand in fluorescent gear, albeit for safety's sake.

This particular moorland valley carries the country lanes to and from the southerly outskirts of Kelbrook, which are car-free save for the spasmodic comings and goings of local residents. You are more likely to encounter a horse and rider than a car and driver here. Kelbrook's affiliation with the horse is centuries old and still held in high regard if the presence of old stone horse-troughs are anything to go by. The hamlet's 'Old Stone Trough Lane' (a left turn upon reaching the village) takes its name from a capacious stone trough on the laneside grass-verge, opposite to a splendid cottage. Into this trough trickles moorland water with the chill and purity of that we encountered on the long and lonely Wycollar road. The old trough also marks the location at which we take one of the three footpaths to 'The Old Stone Trough Inn', on the A56 Skipton New Road; our route is a right (westerly) turn.

Here, on the opposite side of the road to the inn, is yet another old stone trough, complete with an integral high step to assist the rider back onto his mount. No moorland waters trickle into this trough, however, and it must be many a year since a thirsty horse took refreshment from it. Today, the old trough serves only as a convenient litter-bin for the jettisoned rubbish of A56 traffic. There is a frequent bus-service to both Colne and Earby along the A56, for those seeking overnight accommodation. See Appendix X for addresses and telephone numbers.

We must now journey for half-a-mile or so along the A56 towards Colne, which is in a southerly direction from 'The Old Stone Trough Inn.' We are now in old Yorkshire, and our route runs through the farmyard of Great Hague, forcing us to cross the old county boundary back into Lancashire to locate it. Marked on the OS map and indicated by a sign at the farm entrance, Great Hague is a right (westerly) turn.

This stroll along the A56, even though fraught with traffic, is by no means an unpleasant walk. To the west, and clearly visible from our elevated viewpoint, is the huge pastoral valley taking the Leeds and Liverpool Canal on its journey to Gargrave and the Aire Gap. Also clearly visible, although only every now and again, is the protruding stone-work of Blacko Tower, which is said to be a folly built by Grocer Stansfield, and a too-ambitious project by all intentions. It is believed that Stansfield erected the tower in an attempt to see over all the surrounding hills, thus providing one of the best views in the county. He finally relinquished the idea when he realised that 'Old Man Pendle' was a stubborn old Celtic warrior, and one not given to ducking low to permit an uninterrupted panorama of its neighbouring countryside. Once through the farmyard of Great Hague, the footpath crosses a disused railway and continues across the field to the Leeds and Liverpool Canal via two sets of white, five-barred metal gates. Occasionally, depending on the time of year, this field, including the footpath across it, is sown with crops. On my visit the

Above: A pastoral view of Blacko Tower, from Blacko Hill.

crop was potatoes, and a few minutes conversation with a young farmhand confirmed that they would rather walkers skirt any crops that might be present, rather than trampling them. This is no inconvenience whatsoever to walkers and assists the farmer in the following way. Considering that most furrows are ploughed in the north-south direction, thus allowing the sun to shine along their length, one can understand just how much of an inconvenience an east-west footpath across the centre of a field can be when it comes to ploughing. The farmer has to make twice as many turns and it takes twice as long to complete the job. Not only this, but as any seasoned walker knows, footpaths crossing freshly-ploughed fields are invariably and unavoidably strewn with great clods of ankle-twisting earth, which can quickly reduce a

party of robust ramblers into a worn-out group of walking wounded! It is far better to skirt such fields when permitted to do so. If in doubt when you reach Great Hague, ask at the farm for instructions. The farmer's family are exceedingly obliging and will be only too willing to help you on your way.

I left Great Hague with yet another new set of directions and the reassuring news that: "there's an electric fence o'er theer at bottom o' yon field but we've switched it off so tha can get past". I've had dealings before with these battery-operated electric fences when they have been alive and kicking, so be careful! I encountered no such problems this time, however, although crossing the deep ditch here can present a headache or two. These again are seldom trodden footpaths, and any stiles that existed have long-since tumbled into the nearby stream. Locate a lone holly bush, which is directly opposite to the farm buildings of Great Hague across the field, and use its lower branches to ease yourself down to the gravel bed. The crossing thereafter is straight-forward.

Walking from the holly bush in a south-westerly direction,you will see the old bridge spanning a picturesque stretch of the Leeds and Liverpool Canal. The public footpath to the bridge is a raised, grassy track which runs diagonally across the pasture and is clearly seen from the hollybush viewpoint. It leads to a stile-to-stile walk to the bridge.

Here, by the canal bridge, is a good place to settle for a while and take refreshments whilst watching the packet boats passing by. The boats have for a back-drop glorious Kelbrook Moor, a looming, purple dominance which refuses to forfeit its hold on the easterly skyline. One mile to the south of us is 'Mile Long Tunnel', a remarkable engineering accomplishment in the history of canal construction.

Leaving the canal bridge, our path winds to the right, keeping hard by a farmyard to meet a stoned road and a line of three identical houses on the rise. Turn right here pursuing the road over the cattle-grid with its adjacent small mill and rushing stream, from where we have some of the finest country lane walking that I have ever experienced. All the ingredients for pleasurable strolling are here in abundance: fine stands of deciduous trees forming a canopy over the lane, flowery dips, marshy dells and a lively, bubbling stream for constant audible and visual accompaniment. Close scrutiny will also reveal the whereabouts (on your right) of three or four old stone steps leading down to the stream, which in turn lead to an ancient single-arched stone footbridge with retaining walls.

No more than eighteen inches in width, it is ivy-covered and for walkers only, the builders ensuring that no other mode of transport could utilise it as a stream-crossing by erecting three stone stumps at one end. It is a seldom-seen structure of beauty, and situated in a dark section of the woodland, approximately ten minutes walking time from the cattle-grid and small mill.

Country lanes always have their own country characters, and this lane is no exception. Picking blackberries knee-deep in laneside vegetation was a stout, elderly chap, with a lengthy grey beard and a pipe dangling from his mouth. He was so engrossed in his harvest that I was upon him before he realised. "Found anything tasty?" I asked him. He straightened his back from its stooped position, let out a lasting sigh, and looked sky-wards at the tree canopy. Then, and with hand on heart, he turned round to reveal his drained face. "Tha knows how for't' gi' a fella heart attack wi' snakin' up like that". I apologised and added that country dwellers usually spotted me before I saw them. "How can I spot thi", he said "wi' mi yead buried in yon braml's?" The smoke rising from the bowl of his pipe corresponded with each word that left his lips, and the smell of his tobacco suggested that a few home-grown herbs had found their way into his pouch. "Anyway", he remarked, "whats tha' doin' up these parts?" Before I could fully reply he interrupted with; "Where's come from? I know tha's not from round here, but I can tell wi' road tha talks tha's from Lancashire some-weer". It was time to explain about my old county boundary walk again, and that I was walking from Mossley to the Duddon Estuary. "Tha's come from o'er Mossley way!" he said, looking absolutely astonished.

"Bloody-hell owd fettler", he said in an admiring tone of voice. "Tha's fair legged it then today!"

I left him with the illusion that he had been speaking to a super marathon man with the ground-covering capacity of the "Roadrunner' cartoon character. Before I departed, however, I peeped into his bucket of fresh, fruity gatherings.I spotted blackberries, raspberries, crab-apples, and what appeared to be rose-hips. What a pie that selection of fruits should make! Or were they, as I strongly suspected,fresh ingredients for a potent country brew?

Country lanes, it appears, not only have country characters, they also have small country churches. The one we encounter to our left along this particular lane is quite beautiful, and its great appeal stems from its diminutive simplicity. Constructed in 1822, 'Mount Pleasant Methodists' Church', has the dimensions of a small country cottage. Save for its black wrought-iron hand-rail on the steps leading up to the doorway, it is painted in unassuming white emulsion. Although of modest construction, I would venture to suggest that here is one place of worship which isn't suffering a dwindling congregation.

The little white church heralds the end of this sylvan country lane, and the beginning of more open countryside. Just ahead is Barnoldswick Road and the embankment of Whitemore Reservoir. We turn left at the lane's end, following Barnoldswick Road for a short distance, where we see a sign : "Blacko-2 miles", and directing us to the right. An easy way to explain the route is to follow hard by the reservoir embankment throughout its entire length.

Blacko Tower is now forever on the skyline, and 'PRIVATE - NO ACCESS' notices are in such profusion on the grassy embankment of Whitemore Reservoir that one can be excused for believing that the British Waterways Board are growing them from seed!

Leaving the treeless, barren banks of Whitemore Reservoir, we pursue the lane to its cross-roads, passing Sunnybank Farm (marked on the OS map) on our right. At the drive of Sunnybank Farm we can look back over lush cattle pastures at the splendid scenery from whence we came, noticing as we scan the horizon that it is still the purple mass of Kelbrook Moor that other easterly hills must look up to.

'Barrowford - Gisburn Track',proclaims a sign at the cross-roads. The farm directly to the fore is Pasture Head Farm (again, marked on the OS map) where we can stand at its gate and place one foot in old Lancashire and the other foot in old Yorkshire, if we so desire. My own deepest desire, however, at this point in our journey was to set my feet at the bar of 'The Cross Gaits Inn,' which is just one mile away in the Barrowford direction and a left turn along the lane.

'S.J.E. Good Ale to Morrow for nothing. A.D. 1736', predicts an insignia over the inn's doorway. Inside you will discover it to be a typical old English country tavern, with little rooms, each with its own log fire and an atmosphere which tempts the taste-buds to blossom. Also, take note: the aroma drifting from the small kitchen is a force with which the weight-watcher will have to reckon! The inn's name of "Cross Gaits" refers to the cross-roads here, although it is interesting to note the changed spelling of the word, 'gait', to the gate of the bleaker Pennines through which we have travelled. Gait is an old English word meaning 'to go', hence, some ramblers wear a covering over their ankles, or gaiters, when they set out along the road. A person is said to walk with a gait when he walks with a forward posture at speed. Gate, on the other hand, is old English for a mountain pass or defile, or an entrance to a town. See the word 'gate' in an open country context, and the wayfarer of old knew at a glance that he was in for a rigorous journey through mountain and moor, whereas 'gait' told him of a much more pastoral landscape and easier going. Two little words which mean a lot, and not only to the packhorse man of yesteryear, but also to the country-goer of the present time who is embarking on an unfamiliar route. Gait or gate also sounds much more romantic than the A56 or the B6245!

With a couple of pints of Burtonwood bitter under my belt, I left 'The Cross Gaits Inn' for the short stroll across pasture fields to Blacko village. Time was pressing and I wanted to end the day in the Pendle hamlet of Barley, if possible. 'Public Footpath to Gisburn Road', is the footpath sign to look for, the sign itself being situated just across the lane from the inn, to the west or your right as you leave the premises.

The footpath abrupts at a stile and a stoned lane close to an appealing small, white cottage. Turn right along the lane to pursue it around the left-hand bend, from where you will see the white cottages of Blacko village nestled in the valley below; you will also see the huge, rounded and scarred bulk of Pendle Hill's 'Big End.' This is our first really awe-inspiring view of the 'Old Man,' and seeing him suddenly like this, steep-sided, sleek and striving for the stars, immediately makes sense of all the poems, doggerels and vast array of verses that writers both past and present have been inspired to write about this ancient Celt. His Celtic air of mystery and many climactic moods not only

influenced patrons of the acceptable arts, but also those of the black art, as the early 17th century parson-poet, Richard James, pointed out in his poignant doggerel:

"Pendle Stands,
Rouwnd cop, survaiying all ye wilde moore lands,
And Malkin Toure, a little cottage where
Reporte makes caitive witches meete to swearr
Their homage to ye divell, and contrive
The deaths of men and beasts..."

We have arrived in Pendle's famous witch-country, of which, in 1634, Sir William Pelham told Lord Conway: " The greatest news from the country is of a huge pack of witches, which are lately discovered in Lancashire, whereof 'tis said, nineteen are condemned, and that there are at least sixty already discovered, and yet daily there are more revealed".

Such weird and wonderful tales of early 17th century Pendle witchcraft, combined with beautiful villages which have hardly changed since the witches themselves lived there, deserve thorough investigation by today's explorer. At Blacko, the old county boundary makes an acute turn to the north-west in its apparent eagerness to 'wet its feet' in the waters of Ings Beck and the River Ribble. We, on the other hand, will visit each of the local villages with a history of Pendle witchcraft, which means a south-westerly journey to Roughlee and Newchurch-in-Pendle, from where we will turn north-west for Barley and the summit of Pendle

Facing Page: Lancashire at its darkest. The grave of witch Alice Nutter, in the churchyard of St Mary's Church, Newchurch in Pendle. Note the skull and crossbones on the slab gravestone, designed thus to prevent the devil's disciple escaping her tomb. Also buried here are other members of the Nutter family.

Hill, to drop into Downham. Here we will re-locate the old county boundary.

From our Pendle Hill viewpoint at Blacko, follow the lane down to the hamlet's main road. Turn right here and locate the post-office, which is a walk of 100 yards. Take the footpath here, which is sign-posted, 'Public Footpath - Water Meetings', down to the bridge spanning Pendle Water. It is best to consult both map and compass to negotiate this route, taking a south-westerly reading from the bridge. Alternatively, following Pendle Water against the flow and towards its source will take you into Roughlee. This is also a very pleasant walk along a fine trout river, through glorious sylvan countryside. It is so beautiful here that its popularity has increased ten-fold over the last few years, with the inevitable result that footpaths criss-cross the terrain in mind-boggling confusion. This makes a mockery out of any attempt to explain precise directions!

No matter how picturesque and pleasurable the Pendle Water route to Roughlee, the hamlet itself is best viewed from the upper reaches of the hills, from where it still retains some of its 17th century charm. Dominating the village scene is magnificent Roughlee Hall, once the home of witch Alice Nutter, who was hanged on Gallows Hill, Lancaster, on August 20, 1612, for assisting in the killing by witchcraft of one Henry Mytton. She is buried in the churchyard of the Church of St. Mary, Newchurch-in-Pendle, and her gravestone bears a skull and crossbones. A landowner, said to be a devout Catholic and undoubtedly an extremely wealthy lady, many believe that Alice Nutter was the victim of a conspiracy by some of her husband's tenants, the Chattox family, who held a grudge about the amount of rent they were

paying. Anne Chattox had confessed to the murder by witchcraft of Robert Nutter, and made sure that Alice accompanied her to Gallows Hill by implicating her in the Henry Mytton murder. Not only this, but one of the main prosecuting Magistrates was Roger Nowell of Read, who, in the previous year, had been involved in a legal dispute with Alice Nutter over estates boundaries. He lost the case, and a considerable amount of money in the process, which probably did little to enhance Alice Nutter's chances of a fair trial.

The only witch to be seen in Roughlee today is the one on 'The Bay Horse Inn.' She is sitting astride her broom with her faithful black cat close at hand. This type of insignia has been taken up by most of the Pendle villages, which also sell (for around £2.00 a time) witch dolls and other souvenirs aimed at the tourist trade.

Witchcraft was rife in 16th and 17th century Lancashire, although the publicity given to the 1612 and 1634 trials of Lancashire witches ensured that it is the Pendle witches that are best-known today, certainly in Laneashire. The Pendle witches of 1612 were under the leadership of 'Old Demdike,' or Margaret Southern, who had her headquarters in an old delapidated barn known as Malkin Tower in the Pendle foothills. She firmly believed in her powers to perform the magic necessary for all manner of misdoings, like all others involved in the black art, and her range extended beyond Pendle to wherever her 'craft' was required. "Cast out All Witches and Devils which have Lately Annoyed these Parts", urges a notice in the 'Black Bull Inn' at Belmont, near Bolton, which refers to a visit by Old Demdike and her associates. It goes on to tell of her 'Evil Angels' and their 'Accurstations of the

Above: The village of Roughlee, with the Bay Horse Inn bearing its witch insignia.

Innocent'.

One 17th century case of Pendle witchcraft concerned a poor, hapless fortune-teller, who the witches had blamed for a succession of mishaps in the countryside, including the souring of milk and the loss of cattle. In order to rid themselves of this undesirable visitor, a coven of witches performed this gruesome ceremony. First, a live cock chicken stuffed with hundreds of pins was burned alive. A boiling of oatmeal mash was then prepared and allowed to set, when the name of the fortune-teller was inscribed upon it. Amidst murmurings of incantations the oatmeal cake was cast on the fire and burned until black. An eye-witness stated that moaning sounds could be heard above the noise of the raging storm outside, who the witches believed to be the fortune-teller writhing in agony from the spells cast upon him. Whether or not it was the fortune-teller isn't known for certain. What is certain is that he died within the week!

Another piece of Pendle black magic is more of a lament of love than a ditty of death: "I, Naphumuhytor Tetragrunatan desire you all by your powers to gard 'X' from all evil spirits and from bad wishes, fairies and nightmare, and from all disorders, and give him good elth and store of welth all his days ... Oh Lord, Amen".

Apart from the sordid aspects of 16th and 17 century witchcraft, there was also a healthier belief in the medicinal properties in herbs and contributed its services free to the sickly poor. The likes of Old Demdike had a profound knowledge in herbal medicine, and this particular old lady, it is said, could successfully treat bronchitis, running ulcers and external sepsis in less time than it took the doctor to festoon the patient in leeches. In the eyes of the authorities, of course, the powerful antiseptic qualities in her garlic preparations were attributed to the doings of the devil, especially when they witnessed a once-hacking bronchitic restored to full health, for example. The old saying that 'The devil looks after his own', was not taken as lightly as it is today and, as often as not, the patients of Old Demdike and company were also accused of being witches, which forced them to abandon what might have been simple but sound liveli-hoods in favour of a fugitive exis-tence. And so it was until 1871, when the last witchery trial was held in Manchester.

Old Demdike died whilst impris-oned in a dungeon at Lancaster Castle. Some say she was 61 years old, while others claim that she was 81 years old. Whatever her age, her premature death cheated Lancaster's population of this particular Hanging Day's 'star attraction', for up to 6,000 spectators would hustle and jostle each other on Gallows Hill for a closer view of the entertainment. Hanging Day was a public holiday in Lancaster. The witches hanged on that fateful day in 1612 were Anne Chattox, Anne Redfearn, Elizabeth Device, James Device, Alison Device and Alice Nutter. They were taken from Lancaster Castle in the early hours of the morning to 'The Golden Lion Inn', where all condemned pris-oners were permitted a traditional 'stiff drink.' From the inn, they were taken by horse-drawn cart to Gallows Hill and hanged before a huge crowd. Only one of the accused, Margaret Pearson, escaped the death sentence, and she was subjected to the humilia-tion of the pillory: "You shall stand upon the Pillarie in open Market at Clitheroe, Padiham, Whalley and Lancaster foure Market dayes - there you shall confess your offence". To make sure that she confessed of her offence, a paper hat telling of her past evil ways was placed on her head for all to see. She was then imprisoned for one year and bound thereafter in the shadow of the gallows to live a Christian and virtu-ous life, banishing the devil from her soul forever.

Today, the Pendle District paints a rather glamorous picture of its history of witchcraft, although the reality of the situation was quite a different story. In 1613, London attorney Thomas Potts, who had been commis-sioned to write the official account of the witchery trials, published his book, 'The Wonderful Discovery of Witches in the County of Lancaster'. He describes Elizabeth Device as: "...a preposterious mark in nature, even from her birth, which was her left eye standing lower than the other, the one looking down, the other looking up". The Pendle witches were poor wretches living in hovels, and were forced to pay fines to the church for not attending services even though they hadn't the money to clothe themselves. One witch told how she was, "without any apparel saving her smock". It is, perhaps, hardly surprising that they turned their backs on the church and looked elsewhere for spiritual guidance.

The church of the time was thereby encouraging the very evil it was trying to eradicate, and the death sentence issued to convicted witches did little to dampen enthusiasm for the black art. Nicholas Assheton of Downham, when asked whether or not he believed in witches, replied: "Not believe in witches ...! Why, Pendle Forest swarms with witches. They burrow into the hillside like rabbits in a warren".

In the years following the 1612

witchery trials, witchcraft in Pendle grew to mammoth proportions. Travellers, save for hardy, adventurous types, avoided the area "like the devil himself" lest they were confronted by a begging witch, and not possessing the financial resources to supply the demand for money, became a model for a 'picture of clay.' Old Demdike explained in detail how such sorcery worked: "The speediest way to take a man's life away by Witchcraft is to make a picture of clay, like unto the shape of the person whom they meane to kill and dry it thorowly: and when they would have them to be ill in any one place then take a Thorne or Pinne and pricke it in that part of the Picture: and when you would have the whole body to consume away then take sayd Picture and burne it and so thereupon by that meanes the body shall die."

Old Demdike's daughter, Elizabeth Device (pronounced 'Davies'), was a 'dab-hand' at making clay pictures, and this she did for her mother on several occasions. One day, so the story goes, Elizabeth was minding her own business when one John Robinson of Barley accused her of having an illegitimate child. Elizabeth didn't take too kindly to this degrading allegation and, rather than making a clay picture for her mother to use, she made one of her own, taking much time and trouble to gain a true likeness. The clay picture was of John Robinson, and on seeing him walking down a lane Elizabeth barred his way, forcing him to stop. She then took the clay picture from her pocket and, before John Robinson's eyes, crushed it in her hand, letting the shattered bits of clay trickle through her fingers. On the third day, John Robinson, formerly a healthy man, suddenly died!

The stories of Pendle witchcraft are many, yet when one visits this breathtakingly beautiful part of Lancashire, it is difficult to imagine that such dire deeds of the devil could have ever taken place here. Not many years after the 1634 Pendle witchery trials, in which none of the accused were convicted, George Fox struggled to the summit of Pendle Hill, although he went forth with a Hallelujah in his eye and returned to form the Quaker movement. He wrote of his ascent in 1652: "We passed on, warning peoples as we met them of the day of the Lord that was coming upon them. As we went I spied a great hill called Pendle Hill and was much moved by the Lord to go atop of it. I went with much ado - it was so steep. The Lord let me see atop of the the hill in what places he had a great people to be gathered. As I went down the hillside I found a spring of water and refreshed myself".

Shortly, we too will follow in the footsteps of George Fox, although first we must visit Newchurch-in-Pendle and Barley, the directions to both hamlets from Roughlee being well signposted along the country lane. Newchurch-in-Pendle is an unspoiled village with an inn, 'The Lamb Inn,' and its old church set back and virtually hidden from view behind a cluster of white cottages. There is also a 'witch shop' here for those with a want for souvenirs. There was a Chapel-of-ease on the site of the church in 1250, which provided rest and replenishment for tired, hungry wayfarers of the day. The present Church of St. Mary dates from the mid-16th century, although only the tower remains from that period, the remainder having being re-built in 1740. The builders of old, realising that Newchurch-in-Pendle was the hub of Pendle witchcraft, took no chances when it came to protecting themselves from the incanta-

tions of Satan's followers. On the western face of the tower is an oval-shaped stone known as the 'Eye of God', which the builders set into the stone-work to watch over and hopefully protect the villagers from the attention of witches. The grave of Alice Nutter is situated hard by the south wall of the church, and is marked by a flat stone, supported by six pillars. Adjoining it is a much smaller headstone, with other members of the Nutter family inscribed upon it. It was common practice to bury witches under huge, flat stones in this manner, so they couldn't escape their tombs to continue their mischief in the after-life.

During my visit to Newchurch-in-Pendle, I was almost accused of grave-robbing! My camera had consumed its film, so I settled behind a gravestone, in the subdued sunlight, to load with fresh stock. Suddenly, a thundering voice shattered the serenity of the small churchyard: "Hey!" the voice screamed, which made a close-by singing robin dart for cover. "What are you up to?" it bellowed. I looked up to see what turned out to be the church caretaker, bounding along the narrow path towards me, his heated disposition complementing the fire in his eyes. "What are you doing down there?" he said as he approached, panting profusely. "I'm just changing the film in my camera", I replied, whilst trying to look as innocent as I possibly could in such a compromising situation. "Oh", he said. "I thought you were up to no good. I'm the caretaker and I have to keep my eyes open". A few minutes discussion with the conscientious caretaker, which included my county boundary pilgrimage, brought an invitation to coffee at the schoolhouse

and a guided tour of the church grounds. "Try and be as quiet as you can in here", he remarked, as he left me alongside Alice Nutter's grave!

I left Newchurch-in-Pendle beneath a pastel blue sky or, as a lady resident walking her Yorkshire terrier described it, "a spell of extra-ordinary good weather for these parts". Deep blue with not even a wisp of cumulus to be seen, the glorious sky brought to mind the amateur weather-forecaster once again, many of which still look to Old Man Pendle for a local summary. The Tudor traveller, William Camden, believed that: "Pendle Hill had an infallable prognostick of rain when the top of it is black and cloudy". This coincides with an old Pendle verse given to the hill's meteorological capabilities:

"When Pendle wears a wooly cap,
All the farmers can take a nap.
When Pendle wears a darkened hood,
We know the day will not be good."

Pendle Hill must be the county's largest barometer, and is, as Stukeley noted on a dismal day in 1725: "A vast, black mountain which is the morning weather glass of the country people".The Hill becomes bigger and bigger as you approach Barley, which you enter via a tree-clothed lane to be serenaded by the rippling rhapsody of Pendle Water, which cuts across country from Barley to Roughlee, missing Newchurch-in-Pendle. Walkers with an eye for wild flowers will notice the environmental changes taking place, how the cotton-sedge of the acid bog has suddenly left the land and how the limestone-loving species are invading it. The temperature will have risen that few degrees that can make the difference between a shiver and a warm glow, for which you can thank the towering north-westerly barrier of Pendle Hill and the heat generated by a flourish-

Facing page: The village of Barley, with Pendle Hill looming in the background. This is the heart of Lancashire's witch country!

Above: Barley marks the point at which we enter an Area of Outstanding Natural Beauty, and thus it remains for the remainder of the walk.

ing fauna. Sweeter air and, so some authorities insist, prettier villages are also other features of Lancashire's limestone country.

Barley began its life in the early 14th century, when it was known as Bareleigh, meaning an infertile meadow. It was also close to Barley, on the windy slopes of Pendleside, that the Demdike and Chattox families lived, weaving their webs of witchcraft over the whole Pendle countryside. Witches, however, were only a part of Barley's turbulent history, with sheep-stealers and a highwayman named Annel adding their contributions to local tradition. Annel gave his name to Annel Cross, which stood near the Twiston Crossroads to mark the site of the gibbet upon which the highwayman met his Maker. We know Twiston Crossroads today as the four lanes to the north of the hamlet which serve Downham, Rimmington, Blacko and Barley. The last time that the gibbet was set up here was in the 1840s, when a troublesome sheep-stealer was caught, hanged and then unceremoniously buried on Twiston Moor.

Today, Barley is a village which caters heart-and-soul for the tourist, particularly families, and provides a car-park, public conveniences, public telephone and a small play area for children, all occupying space close to Pendle Water, and opposite to 'The Pendle Inn'; there is also a fine restaurant here and a bus-service to outlying towns. There are no shops in Barley.

For those wishing to scrutinise the Pendle villages, Barley makes an excellent bed and breakfast centre. I must admit to falling in love with Pendleside and its people, which prompted me to abandon the rigours and long nights of September camping for the centrally-heated comforts of overnight accommodation. I stayed for two nights at Barley Green Farmhouse, which is a completely renovated, 200-years old house of three stories, with every modern facility one could desire, including an excellent library to interest walkers. Owned and managed by Tony and Helen Hedges, who pride themselves on their home-cooked food and cater for vegetarians, I can fully recommend the farmhouse for a touch of inexpensive luxury along the way. Barley Green Farmhouse is situated just 50 yards from the Village Hall, and to your right along the lane servicing Ogden Reservoirs

Just along the lane from Barley Green Farmhouse lives Adam Nutter, one of several descendants hereabouts of the witch, Alice Nutter. I met him while he was walking his two greyhounds along the lane to Ogden Reservoirs, from where I was returning in haste to quench a thirsty throat in 'The Pendle Inn.' "Is Jack Duckworth fishing a reservoir?" asked Adam. I could confirm that he was, and the plump rainbow trout that I produced from my anorak pocket also confirmed that he was enjoying

some measure of success. I explained to Adam that I had just photographed Jack Duckworth in the process of landing the fish, and that he had given it to me for my supper. He cast an eye over the trout and gave his appraisal: "It's worth takin' home is that. It'll go down well wi' a few chips after a pint or two".

I subsequently placed the fish in the capable culinary hands of Helen Hedges at the farmhouse, and proceeded to the inn. Having been informed that a folk group performs here occasionally, and that they might be appearing on this particular evening, I entered the inn with high hopes of some compatible country entertainment. Whilst awaiting for their arrival, I asked a lady serving behind the bar what their repertoire consisted of. "Well", she replied, "they sing 'A Big, Black Greyhound Dog called Bob' and 'Chicken on a Raft', and loads of others that I just can't think of at the moment". Surely, thought I, a folk group with a list of titles in that vein can't be all bad?

Enter Archie McCully (guitar), Andy Clayton (concertina and melodeon), Ken Clapperton (mandolin), Les Leverington (mandolin and tin whistle) and Ray Perry (guitar). Once fully fortified with gin and tonics and pints of bitter, this, in Archie McCully's words, "load of old folkies with nothing better to do" threw themselves into 'The Midnight Special' with a decibel rating that pulverised the place. And so it was for the remainder of the evening, a non-stop jamboree enjoyed by everyone, and one that Christmas Eve would find hard to improve upon. On the following morning, Archie McCully and I crossed paths once again. I was taking my hang-over to the summit of

Facing page: Blackburn's Jack Duckworth takes a plump rainbow trout from Lower Ogden Reservolr, Barley.

Pendle Hill   he was taking his own headache on a business trip to Northern Scotland. I asked him when the band with no name would be performing again at the inn. "No idea", he replied. "There's never anything arranged. We just hope that we all turn up for a session!"

I bade Archie a fond farewell and wished him a safe journey to the Highlands. Still suffering the effects of the night before, I looked up at the high land of 'Old Man Pendle' and the task of climbing it with grave misgivings. Even though the hill falls slightly short (168ft, to be precise) from being officially named a mountain, it more than compensates for this formal deficiency by the severity of its Pendleside approach which, as George Fox explained, caused "much ado - it was so steep". Save for a little footpath erosion here and there, Pendle Hill is as it has always been, and still demands that those with an eye for a magnificent panorama must suffer the same amount of "ado" as those of 300 years ago or before.

"Young Farmers Do It in Wellies", boasted another slogan in another tractor's cab as I negotiated the steep lane from Barley to Downham, although I doubt if the young farmers in question were referring to the accent of Pendle Hill! We pass on our left Ings Ends, which is a farm marked on the OS map, until arriving at sign-posted Pendleside with its warning that, 'YOU ARE AT RISK! ' There had apparently been a spate of car thefts in this area. It goes on to explain the precautions that the hill-climber/motorist should take to keep possession of his vehicle and its contents. This, I am pleased to say, doesn't concern the backpacker, and so I continued along the Pendleside road to read the next notice, which explained that throwing rocks from the heights of Pendle Hill could be dangerous to those at a lower level. Try telling this to the sheep, thought I, which frequently dislodge rock debris with their rummaging in the hill's grassy flank, to bombard the unsuspecting climber in a hail of stones!

Slowly but surely, as each step towards the summit is taken, one of the most magnificent views to be had in the whole country begins to unfold before you. In the valley to the south-east we can take a last look at Barley with its charming off-white cottages, which instantly indicates one of the reasons why the hamlet won the 'Best Kept Village Competition' in 1982 and again in 1983. It is to the north, however, where this aesthetic magnificence is truly revealed, although we musn't forget, in our anticipation of its delights, to maintain an old Pendle tradition. This is to pick up a stone and carry it to the summit, thereby adding it to the pile that is a 7,000 years old bronze-age burial mound. By doing this, those with a superstitious nature will avoid the curse of 'Old Man Pendle!'

Another old Pendle tradition, and one still observed by many visitors, is to watch the sunrise from the hill's summit. In the past, the chosen date for this lofty dawn patrol was June 21, when all sun-seekers, on fulfilling their objective would visit the hamlet of Barley for a welcome breakfast of ham and eggs. As to the origins of the custom, and being familiar with Pendle's past, we need look no further than an early Celtic pagan religion, which celebrated the summer solstice.thus "They don't bother with the ham and eggs anymore", a Barley resident informed me. "It died out during the meat rationing of the last war".

And so to the 'Old Man's' summit, to place our stone on the remains of a

Above: The Ribble valley from the summit of Pendle.

long forgotten Celtic race, and the short walk to the drystone wall with its stile. Over the stile to approach the upper reaches of Downham Moor and there it is - a yawning panorama of Lancashire and Yorkshire, with the latter county dominating the far-off horizon to the north in the lumpy shapes of Ingleborough, Whernside and Pen-y-ghent. After this, it was time to face the stiff north-westerly breeze blowing across Downham Moor, which caused the occasional rain-cloud to scud so low that it grazed the 'Old Man's' pate, releasing a cascade of rain. The rain dampened neither my person nor my admiration for this 'view of a lifetime,' which threw weight behind the 1949 National Parks Act, and the decision to designate the Pendle District and Bowland Forest as areas of outstanding natural beauty.

It is on the Downham Moor flank of Pendle Hill that the change from gritstone to limestone countryside becomes fully apparent. One can see quite plainly the exact demarcation line of this environmental change in the drystone walls of the lower pastures, where white limestone walling abrupts onto that of black, millstone grit. Pendle Hill itself contains a mixture of both carboniferous rocks, with underlying limestone supporting an overlying layer of gritstone. Our walk to the hamlet of Downham is via lichen-covered drystone walls, gleaming white and providing sustenance in their nutritious limestone for many ferns. The change is complete.

According to a competition organised by the British Travel Holiday Association, the hamlet of Downham is the fifth prettiest village in England, with only Castle Coombe, Milton Abbas, Dunster and Finchinfield displaying their charms more favourably. Even though I doubt any Lancastrian agrees with this result (obviously, Downham should have been in first place!) it serves to illustrate to our South of England cousins that Lancashire isn't an industrial mess supporting a population of cloth-capped, Coronation Street look-alikes!

To the north of the village is where ancient Rome rebuilt an already established road to connect their camps at Ribchester and Ilkley - two Roman soldiers are buried by the roadside in Downham. Running along a limestone terrace, here is one of the oldest roads in the country, its origins being embedded in the dim and distant past of some 5,000 years ago. Rather than being known as a Ribchester to Ilkley connection, Irish gold-traders of the pre-Roman era knew it as a section of road that complemented a much more ambitious project - a cross-country highway between the Ribble Estuary and Yorkshire's Bridlington. It forges a route through the Aire Gap and across the Plain of York, a tortuous trek of just over 112 miles.

Bronze-Age Ireland was a supplier of raw materials, such as gold, tin and bronze, especially to the Danes, who specialised in the manufacture of metal tools, ornaments and weapons. From the Ribble Estuary the route used the navigable Rivers Ribble and Calder as far as Read, where boats had to be moored in the Calder shallows and trading supplies unloaded for a rugged overland journey using horse or oxen-drawn carts. Straight over the Nick of Pendle to descend on Downham goes the 'Gold road', pushing through the Aire Gap to join the Yorkshire Plain to head for the east coast and Bridlington. At Bridlington, supplies were re-loaded onto waiting boats bound for Denmark, where battle-axes, arrows, tridents and household items of the day were manufactured for those with the purses to pay for the products. One cannot help wondering what the metal-detector fraternity would unearth along this ancient path of gold?

Downham is indebted to the wealth of the Assheton family for its present unblemished beauty, although some of the credit must also go to the conscientious electricity industry, which chose an underground supply, rather than unsightly overhead equipment. The Asshetons of Downham Hall took over from the first manorial lords, the Dinelays, in 1559, and it was Nicholas Assheton's passion for the Pendle District in general and Downham in particular that influenced his decision to plough much finance into the hamlet's preservation; he vehemently opposed any changes in Downham and usually got his own way. Nothing however, displays so clearly Nicholas Assheton's love for the Pendle countryside than the stern speech he gave to the London attorney, Thomas Potts. Both Potts and Assheton were discussing the witch trials and other topics of local importance, when Potts made the remark that: "Pendle Hill is a great, brown, ugly mass, without beauty or form or any striking character". They were at Whalley Nab, when suddenly and without any warning whatsoever,

Facing page: The village of Downham, on a balmy summer day in 1987. The sound of a trickling brook, bees buzzing in the flowers..........Lancashire at its best.

Nicholas Assheton treated the London attorney, and everyone else in the vicinity, to a defending summing-up of Pendle Hill, letting pour his sentiments loudly and with conviction, and no doubt convincing Potts that here could be another attorney in the making.

"I love Pendle", enthused Nicholas in a thundering voice, " and from whatever side I view it - whether from this place, when I see it from end to end, from its lowest point to its highest, from Padiham, where it frowns upon me, from Clitheroe, where it smiles, or from Downham, where it rises in full majesty before me - from all points and under all aspects, whether robed in mist or radiant with sunshine. Born beneath its giant shadow I look upon it with filial regards. Some folk say Pendle Hill wants grandeur and sublimity, but they themselves must be wanting in taste. Its broad, round, smooth mass is better than the roughest, craggiest, shaggiest, most sharply splintered mountain of them all. And what a view it commands. Lancaster with its grey old church on one hand. York, with its reverend Minster on the other. The Irish Sea and its wild coast - fell, forest, moor and valley, watered by the Ribble, the Hodder, the Calder and the Lune. Rivers not to be matched for beauty ... There is no hill in England like Pendle Hill".

Not every Assheton, however, possessed the responsible attitude of Nicholas. There was a rumbustious Richard Assheton, who was a keen diarist, although the frequent use of the word "tipple" in his writings suggests that he was also a keen and constant consumer of the local brew! Part of his diary reads:

"1617 - July 3. I and Ric Sherborne to Sladborne. It rayned so we stayed and tipled most of the day, and were too foolish. Spt 11d".

"1617 - July 4. Tipled to the afternoon".

"1617 - July 9. To the ale all; Goffe Whiteacre sent for me later to him, and presently back where I laid me downe. I was sicke with drinke".

There was also a Roger Assheton in the ancient family, who appears to have had a habit of upsetting the wrong people. One day he upset the notorious witch, Anne Chattox, and suffered the fatal consequences: it is said that she bewitched him to death!

Downham's church is dedicated to St. Leonard, the Patron Saint of Prisoners, who also had a feeling for country folk. It has a 15th century tower, the remainder of it being rebuilt in 1909, and from its porch said the late Queen Mary, "was the most beautiful view from any church porch in the land". The view that pleased her so much takes in the hamlet's cottage roof-tops, overshadowed by Pendle Hill, and is an unspoiled, old English country scene of great beauty.

Amenities in Downham consist of 'The Assheton Arms,' a post-office-cum-shop and a two-hourly bus-service to Clitheroe. We are once again approaching the old Lancashire county boundary, which lies just a half-a-mile to the north of Downham, flowing with Ings Beck and Swanside Beck, where they meet as a single force to swell the waters of the River Ribble. Now the course of our journey temporarily abandons the uplands to explore two of the most picturesque river valleys in the country.

Author's Note: Chronologically speaking, there follows a gap in my narrative at this point, for whilst Chapter 3's walk was completed in September 1986, I did not commence Chapter 4's walk until the following April. This was planned so that I could enjoy the Hodder Valley wildlife at its best. The walker should plan his or her walk so as to secure maximum enjoyment according to their own favourite seasons of the year, and their effects on the landscape.

Chapter 4:
RIVER VALLEYS WALK

"IT'S down hill all the way from Downham to the River Ribble", explained a roadworker. "and the best way to get to it is by following the lane to Chatburn, where you'll find Ribble Lane by the post office, which leads you to the Ribble Way".

The Ribble Way is a sea-to-source middle-distance footpath pursuing the River Ribble from Longton, in the Ribble Estuary, to the river's source in the bleak uplands of Heaven's Water Boundary, five miles north of Horton-in-Ribblesdale. Initiated by the Ramblers' Association, with backing from Lancashire County Council, North Yorkshire County Council and the Yorkshire Dales National Park Authority, the Lancashire section of the way was officially opened on June 1 1985, by Sir Derek Barber, Chairman of the Countryside Commission and Mike Harding, former President of the Ramblers Association, who kindly wrote the Foreword for this book.

The Ribble Way takes in approximately 75 miles of estuary, river valley and upland moor, although our ramble along the Ribble Valley to the River Hodder only constitutes some eight or nine miles.

The country lane from Downham to Chatburn is a follow-your-nose route flanked for one mile by the course of the Roman or Irish Gold traders' road. At the A59 trunk road, the ancient road lies beneath its modern equivalent to touch the outskirts of Worston and Clitheroe, from where it heads for the lofty wastes of the 'Nick of Pendle.' Our immediate destination, however, is down into Chatburn, which is a partly-industrialised hamlet with a cotton mill, and a limestone quarry to provide road-surfacing materials. It is a village in a hollow, approached from Downham and Clitheroe via steeply descending roads which abrupt onto level ground opposite to 'The Brown Cow' and 'The Black Bull' inns, which stand side by side like bride and groom. "They've not bred as yet", said a Chatburn joker.

If there is such a term as a village being pleasantly industrial, Chatburn qualifies for the honour. Pollution is none existent, and visible signs of the late 20th century in the hamlet's interior are minimal, with architectural emphasis being placed on its 17th century cottages, one of which, The Manor House, advertises bed and breakfast at reasonable rates. Chatburn is the place to stock up with dwindling supplies at the small store. For those suffering the discomfort of the walkers' affliction known as rambler's foot and mouth disease, whose symptoms include, blisters on your bunions and a throat dryer than a cream cracker, Chatburn is the ideal place to put your feet up and sample a couple of pints of the local brew, before the Ribble Way is tackled. I chose 'The Brown Cow', which just happened to be opening its doors as I was passing, and I was whipped back in time to my early teens as soon as I entered the premises.

Rather than the more usual accompaniment of 1980s pop songs that one associates with public house juke boxes, 'The Brown Cow' appears to specialise in pop history, with old classics such as 'Freight Train' by Nancy Whiskey' flooding the atmosphere. "It's many a year since I heard 'Freight Train' on a juke box". said I to the landlord. "Nancy Whiskey". he affirmed. "She was No.

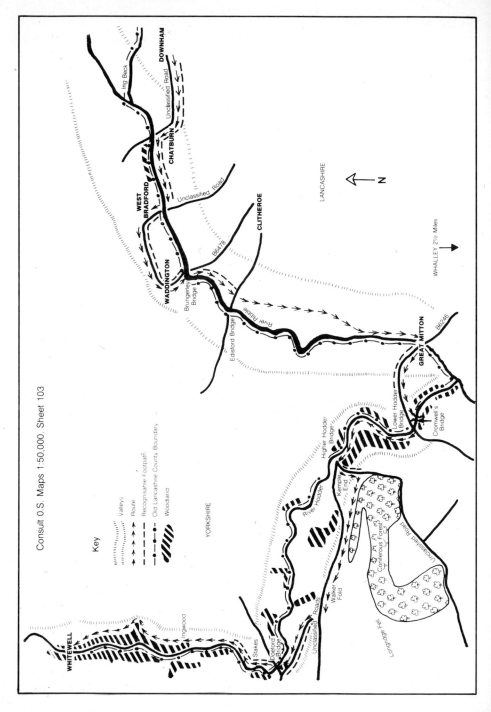

Consult O.S. Maps 1:50,000. Sheet 103

Key

Valleys
Route
Recognisable Footpath
Old Lancashire County Boundary
Woodland

DOWNHAM

Ing Beck

Unclassified Road

CHATBURN

WEST BRADFORD

CLITHEROE

Unclassified Road

LANCASHIRE

N

WHALLEY 2½ Miles

B6478

WADDINGTON

Brungerley Bridge

Edisford Bridge

River Ribble

GREAT MITTON

B6246

Cromwell's Bridge

Lower Hodder Bridge

Higher Hodder Bridge

River Hodder

Kemple End

Coniferous Forest

Unclassified Road

Longridge Fell

Walker Fold

YORKSHIRE

WHITEWELL

Ingwood

Stakes

Doeford Bridge

Unclassified Roads

84

1 in 1958", he assured me, displaying his knowledge and obvious standing in the local community as a pop historian. No sooner had Nancy Whiskey once again drifted into obscurity than 'The Crickets' from the same era filled the lounge with nostalgia. "I once saw Buddy Holly and The Crickets in Wigan", I informed him in a boasting tone. "Did you?" her replied. "I thought he got killed before he came to this country". It's enough to make an old rock 'n' roller's hair turn grey! I bade my farewells, to seek Chatburn post office and Ribble Lane.

A clearly sign-posted right turn, Ribble Lane demands half a mile of walking to reach the Ribble Way, which is a left turn and sign-posted in the first instance as 'Public Footpath - West Bradford'. No sooner has the stile been negotiated than the beautiful Ribble Valley reveals its magnificence, with the shimmering water-course writhing between meadow and marsh 200 feet below the stand of deciduous trees which dress its southerly bank. I have always had a soft spot for this glorious river valley, for its sudden shifts from calm waters to rippling rapids, or from crystal clear shallows to deep, swirling pools. Couple this with its accompanying, unspoiled countryside, so rich in wildlife, and you have the perfect setting to liven a city-weary heart.

The three most prominent bird species inhabiting the water-course are mallard, dipper and two or three colonies of sandmartins, the latter of which find the river's vertical sandy banks ideal for the easy excavating of nesting burrows. In the woodlands, the willow warbler and blackcap are constant songsters, while the lush riverside pastures belong to many lapwings and the occasional redshank and oystercatcher. I have no doubt that kingfisher, common sandpiper and grey wagtail spend their summers on the river also, although I saw none during this particular visit. Constantly in appearance, however, were trout as they struck at surface insects, with the occasional fat chub clearing the surface altogether during a spasm of high spirits. Fishing is strictly private here and under the scrutiny of water bailiff Colin Marginson, who keeps a watchful eye on six miles of river in the West Bradford district.

Formerly a water bailiff on Scotland's River Spey, and a game-keeper on a Yorkshire grouse moor, I met Colin Marginson at West Bradford Bridge. Our mutual interests in photography and outdoor life sparked an instant rapport, and an hour's discussion about the river, and his role in its upkeep. He explained how he believes the West Bradford stretch of the Ribble to be as pleasant a length of river as any in the country, and how reports of otter sightings by visitors are becoming commonplace. "I'm afraid they are mink rather than otters that the visitors are seeing", he explained, "Which is rather disturbing. There are no otters on the river".

A mink in a stretch of river is akin to a fox in a hen-house, but whilst steps can be taken to prevent the fox from entering a hen-house, a river and its wildlife dwell at the mercy of a population of mink. Bred in captivity for its valuable fur, the mink is a semi-aquatic member of the weasel family and a native of Scandinavia, although escapes over the years from British breeding farms have resulted in our rivers becoming colonised by this ferocious predator. Unlike most predators, which usually kill only when they are hungry, the mink appears to delight in the annihilation of all other creatures inhabiting what it regards as its stretch of river. Fish, mammals, birds and even birds' eggs form a mink's diet, which means that

mink on the River Ribble is indeed bad news.

Nevertheless, most news concerning the welfare of the Ribble is good, particularly where the biggest killer of all is concerned - river pollution. I found it difficult to believe how a river in the vicinity of industrial activity including a cotton mill, limestone quarrying and a cement works, could be so pollution-free. "The nearest industry to the river is the cement works", explained Collin "And they're excellent. The firm has invested millions of pounds in a Swedish coal-burning incinerator, which filters out all impurities before they reach the atmosphere or the river. If anything does go wrong, it only takes a telephone call to put matters right again."

Limestone quarrying close to Chatburn dates back to at least the mid-17th century, although the industry intensified between 1830 and the 1960s to provide lime for agriculture and construction. From these quarrying activities has come Salthill Geological Trail, its exact location being midway between Clitheroe and Chatburn, and hard by the route of the ancient Irish gold traders' road - the OS map simply refers to it as 'discontinued quarries'. Salthill Geological Trail is a site of great geological importance, consisting of a series of limestones that were formed about 300 million years ago on the bed of a warm sea. Fossilised marine animals absolutely abound here, and a detailed leaflet explaining the whereabouts of important sites can be obtained from: *The Tourist Information Centre, Council Offices, Church Walk, Clitheroe, Lancashire. BB7 2RA*

"I'm sure that there are more fossils in this district than anywhere else in the world", remarked Colin Marginson. It is certain is that the River Ribble at West Bradford is rich in various marine fossils, both on the banks and on the river bed. Every other river-worn stone appears to contain evidence of this prehistoric sea, with several of the fossilised remains being of the same species found in estuaries and on beaches today. Here, the River Ribble offers a glimpse into the past, to a time before the valley assumed its present-day character. This stretch of the river is also worthy of a little of our time, if not for the 300 million years of history on show, then simply for the beauty and tranquility of the place. It truly is a tonic...

Small arrows displaying the letters 'RW' indicate the Ribble Way route, although we are going to turn off its course briefly to visit the splendid villages of West Bradford and Waddington. Once over West Bradford Bridge take a right (northerly) turn and simply follow the country lane into the village. West Bradford contains a post office, a newsagent, and a splendid tavern, 'The Three Millstones', which is complete with open fire and all of those irresistible trappings associated with the best in country inns - good beer, good food and good company. My participation, however, in the comforts of 'The Three Millstones' was but brief, for at nearby Waddington there are three more inns, each offering fine country fare. A chat with a window cleaner at 'The Three Millstones' convinced me that my intention of having a pint in each village inn was, in these parts, sheer folly. "Your next inn after this one is at Grindleton", he said, "which you should have visited before this one. You could have then come here for a pint and continued to Waddington for another three pints".

Rapid calculation, including the two pints at Chatburn, totalled seven pints in all, which rekindled an occasionally recurring memory of my once attempting to erect a new and consequently unfamiliar tent whilst under the influence of country brew...! That had been an unforgettable experience, for as darkness descended, so did the tent, and I recall uttering those two immortal words, "never again", as the wind sought to take both tent and I to the far side of the moor! A most uncomfortable night was endured, followed by a lengthy and painstaking morning trying to locate tent-pegs lost in long moor-grass, in the added discomfort of intermittent heavy rain! Feeling and looking wet, I swore there and then that this first time would be the last time...

Meanwhile, back at "The Three Millstones, my stay wasn't as brief as I had originally intended. Kindred spirits once again developed an immediate friendship when a party of ramblers noticed my rucksack, and how my flushed face was buried in my now rather grubby OS map. "Can I be of assistance?" asked a lady. "I'm familiar with this countryside", she continued. I once again explained about my county boundary walk. "What a pioneering adventure", she said as she turned to her friends. "He's walking along the old county boundary", she announced, whence they all arrived, drinks in hand to exchange pleasantries. "It must be fantastic to do something like that", remarked the tall lady. I told her that it could be more miserable than fantastic, especially when struggling against wind-driven rain on a high moor. "Persevere", she advised, as she walked towards the bar to replenish her drink.

She returned from the bar with the words: "Here's another pint of that good ale to help you on your way", and placed the drink by the side of my original pint. I thanked her and we settled down around the OS map to partake in another half-hour of pre-planning and re-routing, after which I went on my way.

To leave West Bradford for Waddington is a left (westerly) turn when leaving 'The Three Millstones,' and passing on your right a row of white, ivy-clad cottages. Follow the country lane, again passing on your right a sign for Eaves Hall Caravan Site, and the imposing insignia of a black fox at the entrance to Meadow Head Farm. Waddington is now a follow-your-nose route along the country lane. Pruned, pampered and spotlessly clean - this is Waddington. Architecturally, the village is a delight, with the 15th century Parish Church of St. Helen standing like the guardian of the village, its elevated site permitting it to tower above all but the distant peaks of the fells. Rebuilt in 1901, save for its tower, its attractive setting can be distracting, persuading visitors to linger around the church, its grounds and adjacent gardens without seeking out other Waddington interests.

One of the hamlet's three inns, 'The Lower Buck,' is an unchanged 18th century tavern, where the patron receives his pint of Theakston's 'Old Peculier' through a small bar hatchway. The inn is owned by Waddington Hospital Trust, who use the rent from the inn and that of several farms and houses to support the 17th century almshouses. Originally constructed to house ten widows of the Anglican faith, the almshouses continue a flower rota, whereby each tenant takes turn in maintaining the gardens. It is a tradition dating back to the 18th century, when the tenants had allowed the gardens to run down; the flower rota

was thus introduced as a condition of tenancy. A list in the porch of the small Hospital Chapel explains whose turn it is to perform the task.

Here at Waddington are memories of the Lancastrian king, Henry VI, who, fleeing from his defeat at the Battle of Hexham on May 14 1464, found refuge at Waddington Hall to ease his journey north. He was eventually betrayed by Thomas Talbot of Bashall Eaves and hunted by the Black Monk of Abyntone, whose men captured the king near Brungerley Bridge. The king's hands were bound, and he was made to face backwards on his horse during his journey to London with his feet secured to the stirrups. Imprisoned in The Tower, the Lancastrian king was never heard of again.

Some suggest that Waddington is *too* neat and tidy or, as one visitor bluntly described it: "A landscape gardener's dream, and Nature's nightmare",implying that Nature isn't permitted much licence to choose what should grow, or where. Hart's-tongue fern and various mosses, lichens and flowering plants inhabit the drystone walls of the village stream, and a cottage whose garden abrupts at the stream can boast the dipper and grey wagtail in its list of birdlife. This apart, however, the naturalist really needs to venture forth from the village, leaving behind the trimmed ornamental trees and shrubs for more liberated landscapes. Nevertheless, having said this, one cannot dispute

Dominating the syline at Waddington village is the 15th century church of St Helen,, whilst in the foreground is Waddington Brook, bordered by neatly tended grass and flower beds.Visit Waddington mid-week for quieter moments.

Waddington's stunning beauty, which is substansiated by the hamlet's credible accomplishments in Lancashire's Best Kept Village Competition, with several 'firsts' against its name. It has become a great tourist attraction, each summer weekend seeing its inns and car park packed to capacity. Visit Waddington mid-week for quieter moments.

Waddington's two remaining inns are 'The Higher Buck' and 'The Sun Inn.' In having patronised both 'Bucks' on previous visits, I chose' The Sun Inn' for a new experience. A rather languid mood resulting from my earlier refreshment at Chatburn and West Bradford had indeed submitted to the keen Ribble Valley air, but on a serious note, I should stress that frequent 'bending of the arm' is not to be recommended on lengthy rambles, especially if the countryside is wild and possibly hazardous. On this occasion, however, the route was over level river bank or country lanes;also the inn is the hub of any village community and as I like to meet and talk with local people, I decided to venture indoors.

The hosts of 'The Sun Inn' at Waddington are Peter and Jen Freeman, formerly of Skipton, who had taken possession of this, their first inn, only nine weeks before. It is an open-all-hours establishment, serving coffee and sandwiches during unlicenced hours or, if you prefer, a complete dinner. The menu is reasonably priced, which allows those who have developed a healthy appetite to partake in lavish self-indulgence without 'breaking the bank.' My visit coincided with one of Waddington's mid-week quieter moments, and Jen was busy telephoning orders for vegetables in preparation for the weekend rush of customers. I, like so many other 'townies' before me, have often considered that running an old country tavern borders on the idyllic, although a few enlightening words from Jen soon shattered that particular dream: "We've been here for almost nine weeks", explained Jen, "and we still haven't found enough spare time to familiarise ourselves with the village. Visitors are constantly telling us how beautiful the almshouses are, yet we have been too busy to see for ourselves."

Seek out the B6478 Waddington-Clitheroe road, which is signposted in the village itself. During mid-week, the B6478 provides a mile or so of pleasant country lane walking before arriving at the River Ribble and Brungerley Bridge, where the Ribble Way and the old county boundary accompany the river in a south-westerly direction towards Edisford Bridge. During the last half a mile along the B6478 to the river, you will flank on your right the extensive estate belonging to impressive Waddow Hall, whose continuously crowing pheasants are an audible landmark hereabouts. The hall itself is visible on climbing the stone stile leading down to the river, which is situated on your right at the Clitheroe side of Brungerley Bridge. This, once again, is the Ribble Way and is way-marked thus on the river bank.

History explains that, in the days of King Henry VI, Brungerley Bridge used to be known as Brungerley Stepping Stones, although the stones disappeared beneath the surface when man introduced weirs to control the river, as seen just downstream of Brungerley Bridge on the

Ribble Way route.

Clitheroe castle is the oldest stronghold in Lancashire, its prominent position on the top of a limestone knoll being visible for miles around. Guarding the Ribble Valley, the castle was built by Roger de Poictou *circa* 1186, the Domesday Book referring to it as *Castellatus Rogeri* from the Norman baron who held all the lands between the Ribble and the Mersey. Clitheroe Castle was conducting laws of court long before Lancaster Castle was built, and never in its history as a stronghold had its defences routed by invading marauders. It must have been an awesome, off-putting sight to the invading Scots of the 15th century, so much so that they completely ignored it and focussed their attentions on other spoils in the Ribble Valley! Clitheroe Castle was such an impenetrable defence that war plays little part in its long history, although Oliver Cromwell is believed to have been responsible for a large hole in the east wall of the Keep. Others say that the hole was the doing of the Devil, who threw a huge boulder from the summit of Pendle Hill.

Today, Clitheroe Castle focusses its attention on attracting tourists, with its six acres of land within the Castle groundwork playing host to bandstand concerts, Morris dancing and other festivals akin to Clitheroe tradition. In the Castle House can also be found Clitheroe Museum, which contains many items of local interest Early closing day in Clitheroe is Wednesday, and there are markets on Tuesdays and Saturdays. Local dialect pronounces Clitheroe as Clith-o-rer. More information concerning the attractions of the ancient market town can be had from *Clitheroe Tourist Information Centre, Council Offices, Church Walk, Clitheroe. Tel: Clitheroe 25566.* Hours of opening are 8.45 am until 5.00 pm on weekdays, and 10.00 am until 4.00 pm on Saturdays and Bank Holidays from Easter to September.

Whalley is more of a large village than a small town, and one whose ancient abbey ruins and adjacent church standing on the bank of the River Calder attract thousands of tourists each year. The splendid old church dates from about 1200, and replaces an earlier structure known to the Saxons as' The White Church under the Leigh.' In the churchyard, there are three ancient crosses, each over a thousand years old and believed to be of Norse origin, while a gravestone bearing the date 1856 issues this chilling epitaph:
'Spectators all, as ye pass by,
As you are now so once was I;
As I am now so you will be,
Prepare for death and follow me'.

The construction of Whalley Abbey began on April 12 1296, following a petition from one Henry de Lacy to the pope to re-settle the monks of Stanlawe Abbey in Cheshire, which was suffering ill-effects from an encroaching River Mersey. Henry de Lacy swayed a favourable decision from the pope by explaining that, "the distribution of alms and hospitality would be multiplied and a barren district would receive succour for all time. As long as the world lasted twenty Masses would be said daily for the souls of the pope and the earl". Henry VIII, however, had his own plan for England's abbeys, and the Reformation saw Whalley Abbey practically pulled down and Abbot John Paslew, together with two other monks, hanged, drawn and quartered at Lancaster in 1537. The charge was treason, resulting from their joining

Facing page: Historic Whalley Abbey, built from 1296 and subsequently a victim of Henry VIII's Reformation during the 16th century.

the Pilgrimage of Grace.

Nothing remains of the abbey church save for a section of south wall, a little of the south-east wall and some bits and pieces. The high altar stands amidst restored foundations, and each section of groundwork displays a sign explaining its former role in abbey life. The buildings to the west of the cloister, however, remain intact, and have been restored for use as a conference centre.

An entrance fee of 60p is charged to visit the abbey ruins, the ruinous stonework of which is now occupied by several nesting jackdaws. There are toilets and a cold-water tap in the grounds, and also a fountain trickling from a boulder. "Don't drink the fountain water", I was instructed, "because it's mucky".

Curlew are very much in evidence along the Brungerley Bridge stretch of the river, coasting down from the moors of the north-west and from our forthcoming route over the vast Forest of Bowland. Having spent the winter seeking the far easier pickings on our coastal marshes, the curlew arrives back in its moorland breeding territory in late February or early March and is the first sign that a moor is recovering from winter's icy grip. Little in nature has the ability to stir the senses more than the wild, haunting cry of a curlew as it performs its courtship display over the wide expanse of a lonely moor, or glides effortlessly down the throat of a river valley such as this, where valley accoustics amplify its high-pitched trills. Yet, it is only quite recently that the curlew has been afforded protection from the wild-fowler's gun, before which curlews formed part of the display fronting many a grocer's shop; now there is talk of taking them off that protection list. Let us hope that this never happens.

With curlews, trout fishermen and the butt-end of Longridge Fell for company, the Ribble Way from Brungerley Bridge to Edisford Bridge takes in one mile of pasture field walking, with the route again being waymarked with the letters 'RW' imprinted on small, wooden arrows. However, in summer, when trees, hedgerows and vegetation of all types display luxuriant foliage, the small Ribble Way signs occasionally become lost amidst the tangle of brackens and brambles. When this occurs, and there are two or even three footpath stiles from which to choose, the situation is made worse by the fact that parts of the Ribble Way follow completely new footpaths which haven't as yet made their way onto the OS map. Look for stiles containing a covering of anti-slip wire netting, which I found to be a sound method of locating the way - it also avoids rummaging about in chest-high stinging nettles to discover a way-marker.

Edisford Bridge carries the B6243 Clitheroe road over the river, and is the favourite spot of many campers and caravanners who utilise the facilities provided here. An indoor public swimming pool, a pitch and putt course, children's playground, model railway and' The Riverside Cafe' comprise some of the amenities on offer at Edisford Bridge, where a sign announces that Clitheroe's twin town is Rivesaltes, France.

I prefer the solitude of rambling alone, and whilst the countryside is there for us all to enjoy,Edisford Bridge does appear to have been rather over-planned, with all these leisure facilities packed into a relatively small area. The result is that a once tranquil rural atmosphere has been sacrificed for holiday camp activities, simply destroying the peaceful appeal of the location which is supposed to be the attraction in the first place, in my view.

Anyway, pass Edisford Bridge Caravan Site to locate the Ribble Way stile, where the route cuts diagonally across the pasture to skirt a private riverside woodland and once again take a diagonal course to a stile at the far corner of another pasture. Here, the Ribble Way becomes a stoned track leading to a Lancashire County Council refuse dump; the track offers splendid views of Clitheroe Castle and Pendle Hill. This stoned track leads to Shuttleworth Farm, where the Ribble Way goes through the farm-yard to an open stile on your right at the farmyard's far end. It is here that the River Ribble and its environs attempt to regain the character for which they are renowned, and where the hamlet of Great Mitton reveals its presence in the distance, with the tower of the Church of All Hallows, a magnificent old church built during the reign of Edward III. An interest-ing feature of the church is a 'leper window', where victims of the disease would view Sunday service from the outside; it is also believed that those in disgrace were made to do likewise. Bread and alms for the poor were also distributed through this window.

The Ribble Way approaches Great Mitton via the pasture of the high bank supporting a flank of riverside woodland. It can be a little confusing here, not to mention wet underfoot, when the wrong footpath is taken, leading the walker by the water's edge on what at first appears to be a picturesque route. This lower foot-path is a walk only for the 'welly wearer' however, not the fellboot fraternity, and can lead the unsuspect-ing rambler into all kinds of swampy situations.

To the fore, and on the opposite bank of the river, stands 'The Aspinall Arms,' at the side of which is a long, brick barn. The barn is the clue to the whereabouts of the Ribble Way, which runs alongside it to enter the hamlet close to the 'Old Stone Eating Establishment' and its notice promis-ing 'good informal eating' and 'bite 'n' beer at the bar'. In the village itself, just by the Church of All Hallows, a Tea House serves morning coffee and afternoon teas, with hours of business from 10.00 am until 5.30 pm on every day except Friday, when this cafe is closed. There is also a cafe-cum-stores (next door to the Tea House) whose hours of business are as described above -inconvenient if you pass on a Friday!

The history of Great Mitton dates back to the reign of King John, when nearby Stonyhurst College was a mansion belonging to Hugh de Mitton. Today, Stonyhurst is a college of national repute, and holds the dis-tinction of being the first public build-ing to be lit by gas, the eventful day being February 18 1811. And yet another first in the Mitton calendar is found on the road running from Old Hodder Bridge to Hurst Green, where the tarmac was originally laid by a no lesser person than Mr MacAdam himself. In our case, however, Great Mitton offers a 'last' rather than a 'first' - a last chance to appreciate the splendour of the River Ribble, which meanders through the hamlet at its resplendent best, wide, shallow and with glasslike clarity to imprint a lasting memory on the mind. Just15 minutes walking along the Ribble Way, or the lane passing Great Mitton's other inn, 'The Three Fishes,' brings us to that other splendid valley which carries the River Hodder for some 50 miles from its source at Lamb Hill Fell in the Forest of Bowland.

Follow the lane from Great Mitton, passing 'The Three Fishes' on your

left and taking the B6243 Hurst Green and Longridge road at the junction, whilst simultaneously glancing back at Great Mitton, whose outline fronting a backcloth of 'Old Man Pendle' offers a scene of unchanged old England. However beautiful though the scene may be, your senses must be aware of the traffic on this potentially hazardous stretch of road, keeping as close to the grass verge as possible.

Dipping and rising, twisting and turning, the B6243 contorts itself to Hurst Green and Longridge, although no dip is keener than the one descending to Lower Hodder Bridge and the river flowing beneath it. Next to come into view is Old Hodder Bridge, known as Cromwell's Bridge since the General and his troops marched across it to engage in the Battle of Preston. Cromwell's Bridge is situated just 30 yards or so down river from Lower Hodder Bridge, and is no longer in use. It was here, at Cromwell's Bridge, that I settled down in the sunshine amidst the dense carpet of river bank wild garlic to take lunch, choosing the remnant moss-strewn trunk of a felled tree to serve as dining chair and dining table, and also as a kitchen table from which to spread lashings of melted, runny peanut butter onto thick slices of warm malt-loaf, which is a permanent fixture in my pack. On the shingly shoreline of the opposite bank, two carrion crows were busily poking about, searching every pebble with probing beaks to unearth a tasty insect or two. In feeling sorry for their plight, I took a slice of wholemeal bread from the remainder of a small loaf in my rucksack and, in hope of reaching the opposite bank,

Facing page: Lofty Cromwell's bridge, spanning the River Hodder, near Mitton. A peaceful spot for reflection and thought, and for observing Lancashire's wildlife.

tossed it into the air only to see it fall in the strong current. Both carrion crows immediately took to the wing and, looking like to black cloaks caught in gale, flew down river to a spot some75 yards away, beneath a stand of deciduous trees. I assumed this course of action to be an act of self survival, the crows taking flight to escape what they considered a dangerous situation. I couldn't have been more mistaken...

Whilst following the river journey of the bread through my binoculars, it became apparent that the two carrion crows had not taken to the air through fear, but had employed what was obviously a well rehearsed feeding tactic - the slice of bread beached almost at their awaiting beaks, and was then subjected to a frenzied, greedy attack by both birds! They had calculated exactly where the slice of bread would come to shore. Old *Corvus corone corone,* to use the carrion crow's Latin name, is truly one of Nature's outstanding survivors!

The two adjacent bridges signify our abandonment of the Ribble Way, the old county boundary now pursuing the River Hodder on a northerly course as far as Hodder Bank, two miles to the north of Whitewell. Indeed, the name Hodder is derived from the ancient word *odre*, meaning limit or bound, with the River Hodder once having been the boundary separating two primitive, warring British tribes. It now separates old Lancashire from old Yorkshire, and provides both counties with what can only be described as a naturalist's paradise.

From Lower Hodder Bridge, take the footpath at the Hurst Green side of the bridge, and on the opposite side of the road to Cromwell's Bridge - a small, ash layby fronting the stile gives its whereabouts and you will be walking upriver on the left-hand bank. To your left and fore, standing on the distant rising pasture, is the imposing, Gothic-like structure of Hodder Place, once a boarding school and now converted into residential flats. There is nothing here to blight the eye, nothing save for that intended by Nature, with lush pastures racing down the valley from outlying farmsteads to greet the tall stands of deciduous woodlands lining the Hodder banks. The river is shallow, clear and racy, and obstructed in places with shoals and limestone fragments on which the dipper and grey wagtail rest between flurries for insects. In the woodlands, the sparrow hawk and kestrel find a home, preying as Nature intended on the diversity of songbirds to be found here, the most noticeable being blackbird, song thrush, willow warbler, chiff-chaff, black-cap, and the diminutive wren, whose small size is disproportionate to its ear-piercing song; the song of the chaffinch is carried on every wisp of the wind. This particular reach of the Hodder Valley is popular with visitors, although it never becomes unbearably overcrowded, probably because it is rather off the beaten track, and the lack of parking facilities.

Stile-to-stile walking is now the order of the day, passing hard by Hodder Place where the river emerges from an acute bend; it was here I met a trout fisherman, a police inspector who, in his words, was "winding down from a too-stressful job".

"Where are you off to, then?" he enquired. "Following the river to Whitewell and probably beyond", I replied.

"I have to go to work in the morning", he confided, adding "I do wish I was going with you". I left the police inspector to his last few hours

of pleasure, pondering as I walked that financial reward is no compensation for a working life of discontent.

Passing Hodder Place, the single ash track then bisects the river on your right and a conifer plantation on your left to eventually develop into two narrow and sometimes muddy paths, one taking the higher route along the river, the other courting the water's edge. I took the lower path and encountered all kinds of difficulties, including snagging my rucksack in the tangle of low branches, having to scramble on hands and knees over huge, slippery boulders and, if that wasn't enough, having the footpath fade away completely as it plummeted into the depths of a partly swollen river. It is a frustrating and exhausting route, although it can be great fun for passers-by strolling along the river's opposite bank. "You're going to hang yourself, mister", shouted one young lady as she saw me struggling to free myself from an entangled branch. "Ten to one you end up in the river", bellowed her friend between fits of laughter. All very embarrassing and so unnecessary, and made even worse by the fact that from this predicament I could see the occasional stroller casually sauntering along the upper path in relative comfort. Keep to the upper footpath!

The only advantage gleaned from this disastrous lower route along the River Hodder was the excellent views to be had of common sandpipers and oystercatchers, both species of which make an appearance at Hodder Place and prove to be constant companions from this point until this chapter's end at Whitewell. Their calls are an absolute delight, ringing into the dusk and heralding the dawn as they patrol the Hodder reaches in search of mates, and tasty morsels in the shingle beds. The old sentinel the heron is here also, usually seen perched out of harm's way on the uppermost branch of a stout tree, having detected your approach long before you noticed his presence in the river shallows. In days of long ago, the heron was considered to be the coward of the bird world, although the difference between cowardice and a strategic move to survive wasn't appreciated. The heron is alert, wary of the human-being, and yet another of Nature's staunch survivors.

From Hodder Place to Higher Hodder Bridge the river writhes into a mile-long 'S-bend' interspersed with many coves and spurs. It is this continual twisting and turning of the river which creates the habitat so necessary to its wildlife, undermining limestone outcrops which tumble into the river to from shingle beds, or exposing tree roots to create tunnels in which mammals and birds can find cover. Following each downpour in the Bowland uplands, the umber water flows from peaty Fell channels to dis-colour and swell the river, whence more undermining takes place to claim more of the Hodder's banks, thus widening the river that little bit each time. Over a long period of time, such S-bends eventually become islands, and the S-bend on this particular reach of the river is about half way to reaching that goal.

Walking through a ground cover of rhododendron, wild garlic and bracken fern, and beneath a canopy of ivy-clad alders, oaks, sycamores, ashes and elms, some of the latter of which are in the final stages of Dutch elm disease, we emerge from the Hodder S-bend to arrive at Higher Hodder Bridge and the Hodder Bridge Hotel. The Hodder Bridge Hotel is situated over the bridge to the right, just around the bend. Our route takes the turn on the left, at the stile at Higher Hodder Bridge, to locate the signposted Longridge road.

Below: The River Hodder at Kemple End.

Cottages. This is a steep climb of three-quarters-of-a-mile along a quiet country lane to Kemple End, where the footpath flanking the northerly slopes of Longridge Fell is located. The OS map, however, shows the whereabouts of the footpath as Turner Fold, which isn't even mentioned on the signposts hereabouts. Kemple End is signposted, and the Longridge Fell footpath lies almost opposite and is a right turn between the jaws of a bilberry moor.

For the next four miles the River Hodder runs a private course, thus we must pursue this, the only footpath in our direction, to rejoin the river at Doeford Bridge.

This Longridge Fell footpath begins as stile-to-stile walking, and the finding of a baby's dummy en route illustrates the easy-going aspect. To the north, growing in sodden sumps and hollows amidst the green pasture careering down the valley to the river, is bog-rush aplenty, which is also easy going for a few reed buntings, several lapwings, snipe and curlews. To the south, the going isn't so easy for wildlife, with practically the whole fellside being occupied by an eerie conifer plantation in which I saw not a single bird. Dark, dismal and devoid of undergrowth, such plantations serve only the purpose of the timber trade, consisting of alien Norway spruce and their ilk, planted so close together as to prevent any admission of light to the soil beneath, thus forcing a tall, straight growth. However, on a happier note, I was very pleased to learn that the badger has made a comeback in these parts. "I see the old dog badger pretty frequently while I'm out walking the dog", said a retired bus driver now living in the area. "If you get too close to him he just growls and bares his teeth". Let us hope that 'Old Brock' can sustain his return.

I'm afraid that we cannot sustain easy stile-to-stile walking for very long. On meeting the stile opposite to the first derelict farmstead, conditions underfoot turn decidedly sloppy, and negotiating the stiles becomes a matter of first negotiating the muddy puddles impeding them. Water continually dribbling down the flank of Longridge Fell is responsible for footpath morass here. Rabbits are very common here, bolting to and fro between hedgerow and spinney, and judging by the energy, alertness and obvious rude health of the furry tearaways, the latest more virile strain of myxomatosis recently introduced to the south of England by the Ministry of Agriculture hasn't, as yet, arrived here. May the more potent strain of this disease never arrive in the north.

At the next derelict farmstead, footpath indication is non-existent, although neglected stiles do exist. I became completely bewildered at this point; I did not wish to trespass, but at the same time I did need to press on. Eventually, I was rescued by a gentleman walking his grossly overweight Labrador bitch, which answered to the same of Simone. With dog at heel, stick in hand, and a ruddy complexion that told of many hours spent in the field, I at first naturally assumed the elderly gentleman to be a farmer who was about to tear a strip off this particular trespasser. Then again, I haven't met too many farmers with an overweight dog answering to the name Simone! "No, I'm not the farmer", said the gentleman. "I'm a retired long-distance lorry driver and I have to do plenty of walking to prevent my legs from seizing up". He explained that the last derelict farmstead that we saw was Chaigley Hall, "but 30 years ago we knew it as Owd Lizzy's". 'Owd Lizzy,' it transpired, was an elderly lady of robust moorland stock who lived alone in the hall, and who collected old pots and pans like other people collect antiques. However, Old Lizzy's collection was for practical, rather than ornamental purposes, with each newly-acquired pot or pan having its own permanent position somewhere in the house to catch leaking rain dripping through the ceiling! "It was a cold, damp place to live", he informed me, "and not fitting for a lady of her age. She was a tough old bird was Owd Lizzy".

Now with a set of directions from which to work, I said my farewells to my new friend, who advised me to reach Walker Fold the best way that I could if the stiles proved too difficult to locate. "The farmer won't mind", he assured me, "because he lives in Whalley!" The stiles are indeed difficult to locate, at the right hand corners of the pastures when walking from Chaigley Hall in a north-westerly direction; you will pass an old bath complete with taps which is now used as a sheep trough, and which should be kept to your left. Approaching Walker Fold, the last pasture contains a metal gate (rather than a stile) which must be climbed. Incidentally, Chaigley Hall isn't mentioned on the OS map, although Chaigley Farm and Chaigley Manor are so featured.

Walker Fold is a cluster of farms and stone dwellings and has a public telephone. It is situated on what can only be described as a service road to outlying farms and villages in the west, and is but a 'hop, skip and a jump' from what I consider to be the finest inn so far patronised on our journey. Inns, of course, are a matter of personal taste, but for me 'The Craven Heifer' is the genuine article, completely unspoiled and traditional in every respect. To say that' The Craven Heifer' is situated in the 'middle of nowhere' is an understatement, and what a pleasing discovery it is following the long haul up the steep Longridge road to Kemple End and across the muddy flank of Longridge Fell.

Weekends at' The Craven Heifer' take on a Country & Western flavour, with fans of the music donning western outfits, including guns and Bowie knives, to complement the live performances. I departed before the music started, as I wished to establish a successful and comfortable camp on the lower reaches of Longridge Fell. Nevertheless, even at a camping distance of a half-a-mile from the inn, the hootin' and hollarin' and rodeo rowdy-dow could still be heard into the early morning, carried on the breeze in my direction. At the time of writing, bed and breakfast is not available at 'The Craven Heifer,' although licencee Joan Slater is considering the possibility of providing overnight accommodation in the not-too-distant future.

With 'The Craven Heifer' in view, dawn on the flank of Longridge Fell is a matter of 'being up with the hare' rather than 'being up with the lark'. Dotted at intervals on the valley pasture like miniature kangaroos, first up on hind legs with ears pricked and eyes all-seeing, and then crouched on all fours with busy jaws nibbling the clover, the hare is a natural symbol of grace and speed. Very little, save for a greyhound, can outrun a hare, and even the greyhound can have trouble when a hare is running flat-out. In these parts the hare does well, having no predators with the speed to catch him, unlike Scotland, where he lives in peril of the golden eagle.

Descending the rushy flank of Longridge Fell to relocate 'The Craven Heifer', and in so doing putting to flight a startled hen pheasant, we continue westwards along the service road fronting the inn, taking the sign-posted Chipping road at the junction. This is quiet country lane walking, with goldfinches and greenfinches flitting between roadside hedgerows of holly and hawthorn, and the song of the ubiquitous cock chaffinch gilding the cool dawn air.

We pursue the Chipping road for approximately one and half miles, crossing the course of the Roman road, eventually arriving at a long corrugated barn on our right and its adjacent woodland. Here, an open five barred wooden gate locates the path to Doeford Bridge, which is in a north-easterly direction. A searching eye and a placid disposition in this woodland will reveal grey squirrels which, when it comes to climbing trees, make the monkey look positively slow. I ate breakfast at this point, in the company of several herring gulls which were planing down in V-formation past a rising sun to take their first meal of the day in the Hodder Valley. After having sat quietly for a few minutes on a pile of freshly-cut kindling, curiosity got the better of one grey squirrel which stealthily approached by way of upper tree branches. Finally, it became confident enough to scurry acrobatically down the bole of a tree to continue its assault from the long grass of ground level. However, curiosity cannot be taken for tameness, and my attempt to share breakfast with the creature soon had it bounding back to the safety of the tree canopy.

This particular footpath, which begins as a wide track at the five barred gate, terminates at a ricketty stile almost opposite to Loud Mythom Farm and its beautiful access bridge over the River Loud. What a picturesque corner of the world this is, with the River Loud, only a few ripples away from joining the River Hodder, meandering past the grey stone farmstead and the ascending, winding lane of Little Bowland. It is also well signposted, with our route to Doeford Bridge following that for Whitewell, the bridge itself and the River Hodder being no more than a cock's stride away.

During my acquaintance with Doeford Bridge, the bridge was entangled in a network of builders' scaffolding, with one of its retaining walls undergoing repair. It was Saturday, the builders' day off, which was excuse enough for a pied wagtail to examine every nook and cranny in the rubble and dismantled stonework as if seeking hidden insect larvae or a nesting site. This five-miles stretch of the River Hodder, between Doeford Bridge and Whitewell, must, as far as the naturalist is concerned, rank as one of the best stretches of river valley in the country. My visit recorded no less than 78 species of birds, some of which, like the nocturnal species and several songbirds, were identified by their songs or calls rather than by sight. A full list of the birds recorded is given on page xx.

At Doeford Bridge the River Hodder footpath is located on the far side of the bridge when walking from Loud Mythom Farm and on your left, where you will find a stile. The OS map, however, gives no indication of the footpath we are about to pursue, which follows hard by the river on the right hand bank and passes the River Loud outlet where it becomes as one with the Hodder. Luxuriant habitat begins at once, with a well-wooded island in mid-river and several sand-banks and shingle-beds; the opposite bank is high and almost vertical with a dressing of dense deciduous woodland. Here, on the river itself, were mallard, dipper and grey wagtail, while the woodlands throbbed to the mellow. monotonous notes of the stock dove; all of the woodland songbirds, save for the whitethroat, were also here.

After a mile or so of woodland, we arrive at a small wooden hut, close to a stile, from where two footpaths emerge to do what has become usual on this walk: one goes to high ground, the other follows the river's shoreline. Again, take the higher footpath through the carpet of blue-bells and primroses - be warned, the lower footpath becomes awash after one100 yards or so of boulder hopping!

It was on this higgledy-piggledy reach of the river, close to the hut, that a male goosander took to the air, leaving the river amidst a party of four mallard and a shelduck, which is indication enough to suggest that his mate was incubating eggs somewhere in the vicinity. The goosander is a rare nesting species south of the Lake District, and to see his broad, white wing patches in the skies of Lancashire during the breeding season is a most noteworthy occur-rence. Not as noteworthy, however, although none the less pleasing for that, was my stumbling across a pheasant's nest containing ten eggs, the hen pheasant taking flight from the nest almost beneath my feet to put my heartbeat in overdrive!

The discovery of the pheasant's nest coincided with the re-appearance of several common sandpipers and oys-tercatchers, which traversed the reach of the river just above the tree canopy,indicating that a change in habitat from almost vertical banks of woodland, to flat, open countryside was imminent. Sure enough, close to Stakes Farm, the woodlands abrupt onto level, plain-like pasture, with the river a mass of glistening-white shingle-beds, above which is the river bank itself, no more than three feet high, vertical and sandy, and the home of a colony of sandmartins.

I rested close to Stakes Farm's gate, quite some distance away from the sandmartin colony, to bathe hot feet in a cold river, when out of the blue came a male merlin, our smallest falcon, to see if he could pluck a sandmartin out of the air in a single assault. His wings hissed as he passed by, his sickle shape cutting the cross-wind at lightning speed to scatter sandmartins in all directions. He missed, and must have judged my presence too risky for a second attempt, whence he climbed out of the valley with rapid wingbeats to head south in search of other spoils. It was all over in a matter of seconds, and the chattering sandmartins quickly settled down again to the task of rearing a family...... until the next time!

Here at Stakes Farm, we enter the metal farm gate to continue through the farmyard, although taking the time to notice on our left, just behind the first wooden outbuilding, the Stakes Stepping Stones river crossing. This is the spot where many ramblers receive their second baptism; however I have no doubt that most ramblers, myself included, would sooner receive a soaking than see this beautiful reach of the river marred by the construction of a bridge. Fortunately, our route omits the pre-carious cross of Stakes Stepping Stones to pursue the steep farm lane to another metal gate on our left, where the lane bends to the right. On entering the gate, footpath indica-tion becomes non-existent, although the OS map reveals that two footpaths traverse this pasture, one running to hinterland, the other heading north to locate the river once more. The best than can be accomplished here is to take a northerly compass reading when through the gate, keeping the distant Bowland Fells to the fore, and the equally distant Longridge Fell to

Above: Stakes Stepping stones, on the River Hodder, at Stakes. Great care is needed, if a cold 'dip' is to be avoided!

the rear, whence a half-a-mile of walking relocates the river.

The river itself is once more populated by common sandpiper and oystercatcher, the latter permitting close approach to inspect their immaculate black and white plumage and striking, vivid red bills. To the immediate west the countryside is akin to parkland, with trees dotted here and there on rolling pasture, including many contorted hawthorns, twisted and bent into weird and wonderful shapes by the ravages of reckless weather. At home in this countryside are countless rabbits, which lead one to suspect that, with the close proximity of mature deciduous woodlands, this could be the ideal habitat for a pair of common buzzards, although no large

raptors on broad wings could be seen soaring on warm Hodder Valley air thermals. Lapwings wheel and tumble over these lush pastures, whilst many members of the finch family were also seen.

Soon, Ing Wood, with its habitat of conifers and mixed deciduous woodland is upon us, where the footpath skirts the hinterland perimeter of the woodland to begin a gradual climb to the heights above Whitewell. Ing Wood has shooting interests, as indicated by the cartridge cases littering the woodland's immediate pasture, while carcasses hanging limply on barbed-wire fencing also tells us that the carrion crow isn't tolerated here and that he would do well to move on. This is sheep country, and the sheep farmer and the carrion crow are sworn enemies of long-standing. The magpie too invites the farmer's contempt, for he, like the carrion crow, will remove the eyes from new-born lambs without a hint of self-remorse. Such is the ruthless side of nature.

Following the perimeter of Ing Wood is contrary to the indication of the OS map, which shows the foot-path as crossing the middle pasture on a diagonal course, beginning at the southern corner of the woodland and terminating at the Whitewell access lane. Footpath indication on-site, however, suggests that the perimeter route is the one more widely used by the locals hereabouts, and this is the footpath that I used. Of course, we must understand that it it not beyond the realms of possibility that there are two footpaths here, one of which has been missed by the OS cartographers, as at Doeford Bridge. Whichever footpath is chosen, both bring the walker to the Whitewell access lane, although the longer, perimeter footpath provides added natural history interest. Ing Wood is exceedingly wet and westerly facing, which means that it catches the summer sun from mid-day onwards, thus creating the humidity required by insect life. It teems with birdlife, and contains a diversity of flowering plants, mosses and lichens for the botanist to enjoy.

From the stile at the Whitewell access lane, turn left, walking for 40 yards until locating a metal gate on your right, and the footpath to Whitewell. This is gate-to-gate walking across lush pasture fields. On your right, just after the second set of gates, is an old, richly carved stone water trough, into which slowly trickles icy-cold, clear moorland water, with the quality of that experi-enced on the long and lonely Wycollar packhorse track in *Chapter Two*. It is as fine a lubricant for a parched palate as one could hope to discover in open country, although

please add a water purification tablet to your canteen, to eliminate any risk of a digestive disorder. I washed down my main meal of the day with two canteens of the glorious liquid, and suffered no ill-effects whatsoever.

Directly ahead looms the awesome barrier of fells that constitute the beginnings of Bowland Forest. One mile to the east is the hamlet of Cow Ark, while a mile still further east is Browsholme Hall, from where the influential Parkers conducted affairs relating to the welfare of the king's deer in 16th century Bowland Forest, thus giving their name to park and park keeper. We have also climbed to 812ft above sea level to look down on the village of Whitewell and the adjacent River Hodder. On a clear day, here is a magnificent landscape, with the small hamlet being dwarfed by the huge, gaping jaws of the Hodder Valley in which it nestles, and the tumbling river writhing its way across deep-green pastures from the direction of Burholme Bridge. To the west, across the river and on the flank of New Laund Hill, is extensive forest owned by the Forestry Commission, and containing a diversi-ty of trees, rather than a single, alien conifer species, as is so often the case. It is an area known as 'Little Switzerland 'and, as the guide-book explains, 'visitors tend to return again and again to Whitewell'.

I made camp for the night on the birch-scrub and bracken-clad flank of the hill, my purpose being to capture the dawn chorus of songbirds, and to identify by calls the area's nocturnal species. In the latter respect I had not long to wait: with dusk only sug-gesting its intentions to dim the light, a woodcock began to map out its ter-ritory with its flight call of two frog-like croaks followed by two high-pitched whistles. As darkness descended, the woodcock left the stage to a male tawny owl, whose familiar hooting revealed that its territory was the Forestry Commission plantation across the river. Likewise the long-eared owl, with its dove-like call being a constant interruption in the black silence of Whitewell night-time; occasionally, the wind carried the call of a little owl from an unknown spot in the south-east. I had hoped to hear the reeling song of the nightjar........ perhaps next time.

Dawn broke at 4.15 am, and with more of a 'dawn racket' than a 'dawn chorus,' when a green woodpecker chose to voice its opinion from the high bough of a tree above my tent. I was hidden in the tent, and the woodpecker was thus oblivious to my presence, and henceforth began to live up to its ancient name of the lunatic bird. For those not familiar with the green woodpecker's call, let me explain that the bird has provided sounds for many a 'Hammer horror' film, and to be awakened from a distance of just 15ft feet by this loud, spine-chilling laughter was a shock I shall recall for the rest of my days. Having said this, I wouldn't have missed it at any price!

The dawn chorus revealed no new species that hadn't already been recorded en route along the Hodder Valley, although the accoustics of the valley, and my being above the birds made each song that much crisper. It is seldom that you hear the drumming of a greater-spotted woodpecker *from above* ,or look down onto the grey back and barred tail of a male sparrowhawk, as it darts and dodges between valley trees and hedges in search of songbird plunder. I was surprised to see a lesser-spotted woodpecker in these northerly climes, and surprised not to see a pied flycatcher throughout the whole Hodder Valley length, which goes to show that, in natural history, one

cannot always expect to see the expected! What was expected, however, and guaranteed to be present, was morning coffee at 'The Inn At Whitewell', and with that thought in mind I sauntered down to the hamlet.

The gate-to-gate walk terminates at a drystone wall overlooking the magnificent Hodder Valley landscape; walk to the right to locate a wooden gate and the footpath down the valley flank to Whitewell. It is now a follow-your-nose course, keeping the hamlet in view and walking in a direct line to its position, whence you will arrive at a rotten and rickety five-barred wooden gate with a stream running beneath it and a small marsh fronting it. This is the gate leading to the hamlet's access lane...Sorry..!

Formerly known as 'The Fisherman's Inn', 'The Inn At Whitewell' is an old country tavern of 1836 vintage. For a reasonable price, you can enjoy a pot of hot coffee and buttered toast, with morning newspapers at hand. A notice explains that 'home-made bar lunches, afternoon teas, bar suppers and dinners' are also available. Inside the small, white tavern is an old fashioned bar with a decor of fieldsports drawings, such as otter hunting, rough shooting and wildfowling, plus two wall charts identifying wildfowl and raptors; there is also a pool table in this bar-room. There are no shops in Whitewell.

Close to the inn was Whitewell Chapel, once a resting place for Lancaster-bound wayfarers about to tackle the long haul along the Trough of Bowland road. Today, on this site, is the Parish Church of St Michael. Here at Whitewell was also the

Facing page: The Inn at Whitewell, where the Lancashire border walker can enjoy a filling, reasonably priced breakfast, complete with morning newspapers.

Courthouse of Bowland, where the Master Forester dealt with offences against venison and vert, that is to say he dispensed justice to those accused of killing the king's deer as well as those accused of indirect offences pertaining to Forest law.

These indirect offences included the collecting of brushwood kindling, felling trees, permitting livestock to graze on Bowland deer pastures and trespassing with bow and arrow, knife or a big breed of dog. The laws were tough on the poor country folk and carried out to the letter, and woe betide those who: "without lycens keep anie dogg bigger than will go through a stirrupe to hunt deere out of the corne." Stiff fines, and imprisonment in the Castles at either Clitheroe or Lancaster were the penalties meted out to first offenders, with repeat offenders receiving heavy fines and long terms of imprisonment - , occasionally, even the death penalty.

We have arrived in the Forest of Bowland, and Whitewell's postal address confirms this. Also confirmed is that Whitewell boasts what is probably the fairest reach of the River Hodder throughout its entire length. Just a few strides along the lane to the south, below the hamlet's rookery, is a riverscape of great beauty, which, throughout the years, has provided endless subject matter for artists and photographers. The young artist Turner 'cut his teeth' here during a stay at Browsholme Hall, and various interpretations of this scene have appeared on the front covers of books and magazines, and heralded the beginning of several autumns of several calendars! Go into 'The Parkers Arms' at nearby Newton-in-Bowland, and you will see the very same scene in oils gracing the lounge wall. What a fitting last

glimpse of the River Hodder with which to end this chapter, and this first volume of my Lancashire county border walk. We have seen a variety of countryside ranging from the bleak, gritty uplands of the Pennines, through rolling green pastures and purple heather-capped hilltops in Pendle, to the gentle riverscapes of the valleys of the Ribble and Hodder. We have also met a few of the interesting people I encountered on my exploration of this lovely landscape, and enjoyed a pint or two of ale, and several tasty snacks in the various inns and tea rooms we have passed en route. Much more is to come. From this point, our old Lancashire county boundary walk pursues the ancient Clitheroe-Lancaster road as far as Burholme Bridge, where we once again locate the River Hodder to enter the Bowland uplands. Along this road travelled the Lancashire witches and Abbot John Paslew and his fellow monks, all en route to Lancaster Castle, where most suffered terrible deaths. Thankfully, we will travel the very same road under much less dire circumstances..... I look forward to your company.

Facing page: A scene of idyllic tranquillity at Whitewell, on the banks of the River Hodder.

Chapter 5:
INFORMATION

THIS chapter contains a range of information which will be useful to anyone considering tackling any (or all!) of my Lancashire border walk. There are a few suggestions as to where reasonably priced and comfortable overnight accommodation might be found (asterisks denote locations directly **en route**) a list of public information centres and a list of the 78 different species of birds I observed on my journey through the Hodder Valley, for example. Finally, for those who might like to pursue a little armchair research, I have included a bibliography of books consulted during preparation of my own manuscript.

CHAPTER ONE: WALKING THE EDGES
OVERNIGHT ACCOMMODATION BETWEEN MOSSLEY AND WARLAND

St. George's Vicarage, Stamford Street, Mossley*......... .... *Tel*: 04575 2219
1, Springmeadow Lane, Uppermill*...04577 4175
Palinwood House, 105 Delph Lane, Delph*.. 04577 70432
Globe Farm, Huddersfield Road, Delph*.. 04577 3040
Fold Mini Market, Woods Lane, Dobcross*...04577 6491
Higher Quick Farm, Mossley*..04577 2424
The Shepherds Boy, Manchester Road, Standedge*.. 0484 844778
Harrop Green Farm, Diggle*..04577 3937
 Dobcross Village Green, 2/4 persons (Self catering)*............. 0457770992 or 04577 6195
The Sun Hotel, Featherstall Road, Littleborough..0706 78957
The Spinning Wheel, Oak Street, Littleborough.. 0706 79670

CHAPTER TWO: EMBRACING BOULSWORTH
OVERNIGHT ACCOMMODATION BETWEEN WARLAND AND WYCOLLAR

Mrs Pegg, High Stones, Lanes Bottom, Walsden*............................. *Tel*: Todmorden 6534
Birks Clough Guest House, Hollingworth Lane, Walsden* ....Todmorden 4438
Todmorden Edge Guest House, Parkin Lane, Sourhall*............................ Todmorden 3459
Black Swan Hotel, Burnley Road, Todmorden..Todmorden 3507
Queen Hotel, Rise Land, Todmorden.. Todmorden 2961
Mrs. Crabtrees, Stansfield Cottage, Hole Bottom Road, Todmorde...........Todmorden 2979
Mrs. Crossley, Sylvawood, Sunnyside, Todmorden...................................Todmorden 3264
Mrs. Robinson, 68, Bacup Road, Todmorden..Todmorden 5365

CHAPTER THREE: CROSS COUNTRY TO PENDLE
OVERNIGHT ACCOMMODATION BETWEEN WYCOLLAR AND DOWNHAM

Will O' The Moor Farm, Trawden... *Tel*: Burnley 864747
The Emmot Arms, Keightley Road, Laneshaw Bridge*............................... Burnley 863366
The Station Hotel, Colne Road, Earby ....Burnley 842274

Earby Youth Hostel, Glen Cottage, Birch Hall Lane, Earby.
24 beds, standard grade, Closed Thursday nights..Burnley 842349
The King's Head Hotel, Colne.. Burnley 864254
*The Moorcock Inn, Gisburn Road, Blacko..Burnley 64186
*Barley Green Farmhouse, Barley ....Burnley 693438
*The Grange, Barley ....Burnley 64597
*The Post Office, Downham...Clitheroe 41242

CHAPTER FOUR: RIVER VALLEYS WALK
OVERNIGHT ACCOMMODATION BETWEEN DOWNHAM AND WHITEWELL

The Post Office, Downham*.. *Tel:* 0200 41242
Manor House Cottage, Bridge Road, Chatburn*.. 0200 41547
Greendale, Greendale View, Chatburn*.. 0200 41316
Three Rivers Park, Eaves Hall Lane, West Bradford (Camping)*....................... 0200 23523
Fields House Farm, Waddington, (Camping)*..0200 22191
Back Fold Cottage, Waddington*... 0200 22367
58 West View, Waddington*.. 0200 24224
Edisford Bridge Farm, Edisford Bridge*... 0200 27868
Aspinall Arms, Gt Mitton*..025486 223
Old Stone House, Gt Mitton*.. 025486 544
Hodder Bridge Hotel*..025486 216
Higher Whitewell Farmhouse*...02008 254
The Inn At Whitewell*..02008 222

CLITHEROE AND WHALLEY

Brown Cow Inn, Moor Lane, Clitheroe.. 0200 24193
11 Dorset Drive, Clitheroe... 0200 22238
Fairway Hotel, 48, King Street, Clitheroe... 0200 22025
Brooklyn, 32, Pimlico Road, Clitheroe.. 0200 28268
The Starkie Arms, Castle Street, Clitheroe... 0200 22550
Victoria Hotel, Market Place, Clitheroe..0200 22601
19 Abbots Croft, Whalley...025482 3601
36 Abbots Croft, Whalley...025482 2584
Easterly Farm, Whalley...025482 2210
Whalley Abbey..025482 2268

INFORMATION CENTRES

Information centres will provide a range of information, inlcuding details about
overnight accomodation in their area, public transport and entertainment. A large
variety of leaflets are usually available to visitors.

Barley... Burnley 601893
Clitheroe...Clitheroe 25566
Hebden Bridge... Hebden Bridge 3831
Nelson...Nelson 692890
Rochdale.. Rochdale 342153
Rossendale..Rossendale 217777
Saddleworth.. Saddleworth 2598

SPECIES OF BIRDS OBSERVED BETWEEN DOEFORD BRIDGE & WHITEWELL

Heron
Mallard
Shoveler
Goosander
Sparrow Hawk
Merlin
Kestrel
Partridge
Pheasant
Moorhen
Oystercatcher
Lapwing
Snipe
Woodcock
Curlew
Common Sand-
piper
Redshank
Lesser Black
Blacked Gull
Herring Gull
Black-headed Gull

Stock Dove
Wood Pigeon
Collared Dove
Cuckoo
Little Owl
Tawny Owl
Long-eared Owl
Swift
Swallow
House Martin
Sand Martin
Kingfisher
Green Woodpecker
Greater Spotted
Woodpecker
Lesser Spotted
Woodpecker
Skylark
Tree Pipit
Meadow Pipit
Grey Wagtail
Pied Wagtail

Starling
Jay
Magpie
Jackdaw
Rook
Carrion Crow
Dipper
Wren
Dunnock
Garden Warbler
Blackcap
Whitethroat
Willow Warbler
Chiff-chaff
Spotted Flycatcher
Wheatear
Robin
Blackbird
Song Thrush
Mistle Thrush
Blue Tit
Coal Tit

Great Tit
Willow Tit
Tree Creeper
House Sparrow
Tree Sparrow
Chaffinch
Bullfinch
Greenfinch
Goldfinch
Linnet
Twite
Redpoll
Corn Bunting
Reed Bunting
Yellowhammer

78 SPECIES

BIBLIOGRAPHY

The Lancashire Witches
by Harrison Ainsworth *(Gerrard, republished 1965)*

Witchcraft in Lancashire
by Kathleen Eyre *(Dalesman, 1974)*

The Danes in Lancashire
by SW Partington *(EG Morten, republished, 1973)*

The Roof of Lancashire
by Herbert C Collins *(J.M. Dent, 1950)*

Lancashire Plain and Seaboard
by Herbert C Collins *(J.M. Dent, 1953)*

Sika Deer in North Lancashire
by WR Mitchell and J Robinson *(The Lancashire Naturalists' Trust, Ltd. Volume 2, 1971)*

The 'Countryside for Pleasure' series

If you are writing a book, or are considering doing so, and feel that we may be interested in publishing your work, then please let us know. We are always interested to hear from prospective authors. Please write briefly about your idea to:

SILVER LINK PUBLISHING LTD,
The Coach House, Garstang Road, St Michael's on Wyre, Lancashire, PR3 OTG.